MACBOOK AIR M4
USER GUIDE 2025

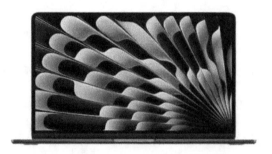

A Complete Manual for New Users to Master the M4
Chip, macOS, Performance Tips, Setup, Customization,
Troubleshooting, and More

STANLEY R.D TEACHINGS

Copyright Notice

Disclaimer

The information provided in this **MacBook Air M4 User Guide** is for educational purposes only. The author and publisher have made every effort to ensure the accuracy of the content, but make no representations or warranties regarding the completeness, accuracy, or reliability of the information contained herein.

This guide is an independent publication and is not affiliated with or endorsed by Apple Inc. in any way.

The author is not responsible for any changes made to the MacBook or macOS software after publication. Users are encouraged to consult the official Apple website or customer support for the most up-to-date information regarding the MacBook Air M4.

All trademarks, service marks, and product names mentioned in this guide are the property of their respective owners. Apple Inc. and macOS are trademarks of Apple Inc.

TABLE OF CONTENTS

INTRODUCTION

What Makes the MacBook Air M4 Special?

When you first unbox the **MacBook Air M4**, you'll quickly realize this isn't just another laptop. It's a revolution in how we think about portable computing. Apple has taken everything that made the MacBook Air iconic and elevated it to new heights, blending cutting-edge technology with the elegance and simplicity that Apple is known for.

A Sleek, Refined Design

One of the first things you'll notice about the **MacBook Air M4** is its design. It's incredibly sleek and lightweight, maintaining the signature thin profile that the MacBook Air line is known for, but now with a fresh twist. This model is available in a stunning new **Sky Blue color**, which adds a touch of personality and vibrancy to the already elegant design. Whether you're working on a project, watching a movie, or browsing the web, the MacBook Air M4's display is gorgeous and offers excellent color accuracy, making it ideal for both creative professionals and casual users alike.

The all-aluminum body ensures a sturdy yet lightweight frame, perfect for users who need to take their laptop everywhere. Its size is compact, fitting effortlessly into most bags or backpacks, but it doesn't sacrifice performance for portability. At just 0.63 inches thin and weighing only 2.7 pounds, this laptop is designed for anyone who values convenience without compromising on power.

The Groundbreaking M4 Chip: Power Meets Efficiency

At the heart of the **MacBook Air M4** is the new **M4 chip**, Apple's most advanced custom silicon to date. If you've been following Apple's transition from Intel chips to their own M-series chips, you already know how transformative this shift has been. But the **M4 chip** takes it even further, delivering an unmatched balance of **power and efficiency** that sets it apart from previous models and almost every other laptop on the market.

This chip is designed with performance in mind, ensuring you can handle anything from daily tasks like checking emails and browsing the web to more demanding activities like photo editing or video conferencing—all without slowing down. You can expect **snappy responsiveness**, smooth multitasking, and effortless switching between apps. Whether you're running multiple browser tabs, streaming movies, or working on a spreadsheet, the MacBook Air M4 handles it all with ease.

The **M4 chip** is also engineered for **energy efficiency**, meaning you get more power for the same amount of battery life. You don't have to worry about plugging in constantly. The MacBook Air M4 gives you the freedom to work, play, or create for hours on end without the need to hunt for a power outlet.

Impressive Battery Life: Work and Play Longer

Speaking of battery life, the **MacBook Air M4** sets a new standard for what you can expect from a thin and light laptop. Thanks to the **M4 chip's efficiency**, Apple has been able to pack in a **long-lasting battery** that gives you up to **18 hours of usage** on a single charge. This is a huge leap forward from previous models, ensuring you can work on a project, enjoy a full day of meetings, or binge-watch your favorite series without constantly worrying about running out of juice.

Apple's commitment to battery life means the **MacBook Air M4** is built for users who need a reliable laptop that can keep up with their day-to-day demands. Whether you're a student taking notes in class, a professional attending meetings, or just someone who loves to travel, the MacBook Air M4 will last long enough to get you through your entire day without needing a recharge. The **fast charging** capability ensures that even if you're low on battery, you can quickly get back to 50% charge in just **30 minutes**.

Handling Everyday Tasks with Ease

The **MacBook Air M4** is designed to handle everyday tasks effortlessly. It's not just about heavy lifting or intensive workloads; it's about providing a smooth, efficient experience for the user no matter what you're doing. For most people, this laptop excels at the basics: web browsing, emailing, word processing, video calling, and media consumption. All of these tasks are handled quickly, smoothly, and without hiccups.

But what sets the **MacBook Air M4** apart is how seamlessly it handles them. Whether you're juggling a video call while typing up an essay or managing multiple applications at once, the MacBook Air M4 offers **seamless multitasking** that rivals much larger, heavier laptops. The **M4 chip's unified memory architecture** ensures that all tasks, no matter how simple or complex, happen without delay. This is a machine that doesn't just get the job done; it makes every interaction feel effortless and natural.

The laptop's **12MP Center Stage webcam** is another standout feature. It's designed to keep you in the center of the frame during video calls, even if you move around a bit. With improved video quality, this makes a huge difference when you're working remotely, attending virtual meetings, or staying in touch with friends and family. The **studio-quality speakers** ensure that audio during video calls, movie nights, or music listening sessions sounds crystal clear and immersive.

User-Friendly Experience

What truly makes the **MacBook Air M4** special is its ability to combine **powerful performance with user-friendliness**. Apple's macOS is known for its clean, intuitive interface, and with the **MacBook Air M4**, it's better than ever. The operating system works seamlessly with the hardware, ensuring that everything just works. From opening apps to switching between windows, everything feels **natural** and easy to navigate.

The **MacBook Air M4** also integrates effortlessly into the **Apple ecosystem**, allowing you to sync and share data between your MacBook, iPhone, iPad, and Apple Watch. Whether it's sending a file via **AirDrop**, copying content across devices with **Universal Clipboard**, or continuing a task on a different Apple device with **Handoff**, the MacBook Air M4 ensures that everything is connected, making it a breeze to move from one task to another.

Even for users who may not be tech-savvy, the MacBook Air M4's simple design and intuitive user interface make it easy to get started right out of the box. You won't find yourself needing to dig through complicated settings or manuals. Apple's ecosystem is built to be approachable, helping you get the most out of your MacBook without any unnecessary complexity.

How This Guide Will Help You

How This Guide Is Structured

This guide is structured to take you from a complete beginner to a confident user in no time. Whether you're someone who has never used a MacBook before or you're upgrading from an older version, each chapter and section is designed to walk you through the setup, features, and functions of the MacBook Air M4 step by step. You'll find clear, jargon-free instructions and practical tips that are easy to understand, with plenty of visuals to make everything even easier to follow.

1. **Beginner-Friendly Step-by-Step Instructions**: Each chapter starts with the basics and gradually builds on your knowledge, ensuring that you're comfortable with your MacBook Air M4. We'll walk you

through the unboxing process, getting your MacBook set up, and familiarizing you with macOS—Apple's operating system—so you can start using your MacBook right away.

2. **Advanced Features for Power Users**: As you become more familiar with your MacBook, we dive into more advanced features designed to enhance your productivity. From utilizing the power of the M4 chip for demanding tasks to integrating your MacBook seamlessly with other Apple devices, this guide covers it all. You'll learn tips and tricks to optimize your workflow and make the most of the MacBook Air M4's impressive capabilities.

3. **Practical Solutions to Everyday Problems**: This guide doesn't just focus on how to use your MacBook; it's also here to help you troubleshoot and solve problems along the way. Whether it's a Wi-Fi issue, a slow app, or difficulty connecting external devices, we've got you covered. Our troubleshooting sections are designed to help you quickly find solutions so you can get back to using your MacBook without any stress.

4. **Comprehensive Tips for All Skill Levels**: Whether you're a tech enthusiast or someone who is just starting out with Macs, this guide is tailored to meet your needs. Beginners will appreciate the straightforward, easy-to-understand explanations, while more experienced users can dive into advanced topics, such as optimizing performance, customizing system settings, and unlocking the MacBook Air M4's full potential.

Why This Guide Is User-Friendly and Comprehensive

This guide is more than just a manual—it's a resource designed to grow with you as you become more confident in using your MacBook Air M4. It's filled with tips and shortcuts to boost your productivity, as well as solutions to common challenges. We understand that every user is different, so we've designed this guide to be flexible and intuitive. You'll find everything from the basics to pro-level features, all neatly organized and easy to navigate.

You'll also notice that we've avoided overwhelming you with technical jargon. While we'll explain terms and concepts when necessary, the guide's tone is friendly and approachable, making it easy for everyone—from the most tech-savvy to complete beginners—to follow along. If you need quick answers or solutions, our troubleshooting and FAQ sections are easy to access and designed to save you time.

This guide is built to solve problems, answer questions, and offer practical advice. It's not just about teaching you how to use your MacBook Air M4; it's about empowering you to take full control of your device, optimizing it for your daily needs, and discovering all the amazing things you can do with it.

Whether you're setting up your MacBook for the first time, looking to master advanced features, or simply hoping to solve an issue, this guide is here to help every step of the way. It's your all-in-one resource, ensuring you'll get the most out of your MacBook Air M4 experience.

By the end of this guide, you'll not only be able to navigate your MacBook Air M4 like a pro, but you'll also feel confident in troubleshooting issues and customizing your device to suit your unique needs. With this guide, you'll turn the MacBook Air M4 into the perfect tool for your personal and professional life.

Target Audience: Who This Guide Is For

Welcome to the **MacBook Air M4 User Guide**! Whether you're holding your first MacBook in your hands or you're a seasoned Apple user upgrading from an older model, this guide is designed to take you through everything you need to know to make the most of your MacBook Air M4. Our goal is to help you, regardless of your level of experience, feel confident and comfortable using this powerful yet user-friendly device.

Who Is This Guide For?

This guide is for anyone who wants to maximize their experience with the MacBook Air M4. No matter your background, we're here to walk you through every step of the process—whether it's your first time using a MacBook or you're a seasoned user transitioning to the latest model.

First-Time   MacBook   Users

If this is your first MacBook, you may have a few questions about what to expect from the Apple ecosystem. That's okay! We'll take it slow, starting with the basics. You'll learn how to set up your MacBook, navigate the macOS operating system, and get comfortable with the built-in apps. With this guide, we promise to break things down in a way that's easy to understand, so you're never left wondering what to do next. If you've always used Windows or another operating system, we'll help you get familiar with the macOS environment and make your transition smooth.

Upgrading from an Older Model

If you're upgrading from an older MacBook Air or a different Apple device, you'll notice a number of improvements that make the MacBook Air M4 a powerful upgrade. The M4 chip's performance boost, the vibrant display, and the enhanced camera are just a few examples of why the M4 version stands out. In this guide, we'll show you what's new and how to take advantage of the latest features. Whether you're looking for ways to improve your workflow, enjoy more efficient multitasking, or get the most out of the new hardware, we've got you covered.

Professionals Looking to Optimize Their MacBook Air M4

For professionals—whether you're working in creative fields like graphic design, video editing, or photography, or you're managing projects, spreadsheets, and emails in a business setting—the MacBook Air M4 is designed to perform at a high level. This guide will show you how to optimize your MacBook for work, making it a tool that helps you do your job more efficiently. From managing multiple apps and windows to understanding advanced macOS features, we'll help you make your MacBook Air M4 a true productivity powerhouse.

Making This Guide Accessible for Everyone

This guide is carefully crafted to meet the needs of all users, from beginners to those with more advanced knowledge. Every section is filled with clear, easy-to-follow instructions, so you won't feel overwhelmed no matter where you're starting from. If you're someone who is a bit more tech-savvy, you'll appreciate the deeper dives into performance, troubleshooting, and macOS tricks. But don't worry—there are no complicated terms here, and we'll explain everything in a way that anyone can understand.

For those who aren't comfortable with technology, we've kept the language simple and approachable. We're not here to confuse you with technical jargon or to assume you know every little detail. Instead, we're here to guide you step by step, so you can enjoy using your MacBook Air M4 without feeling lost.

What You Can Expect from This Guide

In this guide, we'll cover everything from **unboxing** to **advanced features**. You'll get clear explanations on how to:

- **Set up your MacBook Air M4**: Get it ready for use with easy-to-follow setup instructions.

- **Use macOS**: Learn how to navigate macOS like a pro, even if you've never used it before.

- **Optimize performance**: Discover how to make your MacBook Air M4 run smoothly, whether you're doing basic tasks or running demanding apps.

- **Solve common problems**: We'll help you troubleshoot issues you might encounter and get you back on track quickly.

This guide is designed to make your experience with the MacBook Air M4 as smooth and enjoyable as possible. Whether you're using your MacBook for work, school, or personal use, you'll find the information you need to get the most out of it.

CHAPTER 1: UNBOXING AND GETTING STARTED

Opening the Box: What's Inside

The moment you crack open the sleek, well-designed box of your MacBook Air M4, a sense of excitement is sure to bubble up. After all, you're about to experience one of Apple's most celebrated devices—compact, powerful, and undeniably beautiful. But what exactly will you find inside this carefully crafted packaging? Let's take a look.

1. The MacBook Air M4 Itself

The star of the show, of course, is the MacBook Air M4. Nestled in a protective layer of plastic, the laptop is the first thing you'll notice when you open the box. Apple has always been known for its elegant design, and the MacBook Air M4 is no exception. Whether you've chosen the new Sky Blue color or the classic silver, this lightweight, slim device feels like a piece of modern art.

As you gently lift the MacBook Air M4 out of the box, you'll immediately notice its sleek, featherlight feel. The all-aluminum chassis exudes quality, and the Retina display gleams with vibrant colors and crisp detail. Holding it for the first time, you'll understand why this is more than just a laptop—it's a tool designed for comfort, productivity, and style.

For the first-time user, the device is ready to impress. The M4 chip inside promises a powerful, yet energy-efficient experience that will make everything from everyday tasks to demanding projects feel smooth and effortless. If you're coming from a previous MacBook Air model, the difference in performance will be noticeable from the very start.

Why it matters: This is your gateway to the Apple ecosystem, your tool for creativity, productivity, and entertainment. Whether you're a student, a professional, or someone who simply enjoys quality tech, this is the device that will adapt to your needs and elevate your daily experience.

2. The USB-C Charging Cable

Next, you'll find the USB-C charging cable neatly tucked into the box. This is not just any standard charging cable—it's a robust and durable cable that delivers fast charging speeds to your MacBook Air M4. One end is designed to plug into the charging brick, while the other connects to the laptop itself.

This cable is designed for convenience. The reversible USB-C connector means you can plug it in without worrying about orientation, and the cable is long enough to allow flexibility in where you charge your MacBook. Whether you're plugging in at your desk or charging on the go, this cable will do the job effortlessly.

Why it matters: For a first-time user, the cable signifies the start of your MacBook's lifecycle. It's the first thing you'll connect after turning on the laptop, making it integral to your early experience. Plus, its universal USB-

C compatibility means you can use it with other devices, making it a versatile addition to your tech collection.

3. The Power Adapter

Along with the charging cable, you'll also find the sleek, compact power adapter. For the MacBook Air M4, Apple has designed a power adapter that is efficient, lightweight, and powerful. Depending on the region you purchase the MacBook from, you may find it in a 30W USB-C charger, which delivers fast charging to the MacBook while maintaining energy efficiency.

The power adapter is slim, so it won't take up much space in your bag or desk drawer, and it also features foldable prongs for easy storage and portability. It's the perfect balance between power and convenience, designed to keep your device ready to use without being bulky or cumbersome.

Why it matters: For a new user, this adapter serves as a reminder that Apple doesn't compromise on quality—even in the smaller details. Its portability and efficiency will help you power through tasks with minimal interruption. Having a reliable charger is crucial to your experience with the MacBook Air, and this adapter will be your constant companion as you use your device daily.

4. Documentation and Manuals

Nestled at the bottom of the box, you'll find a small set of documents that might seem simple, but they're incredibly helpful to new users. Apple includes a few essential manuals and quick start guides, which cover the basics of setting up your MacBook Air M4, safety instructions, and warranty information. Apple's manuals are typically designed to be straightforward, often using easy-to-follow illustrations and simple steps to guide you through your initial setup.

There's also a sheet that introduces you to the Apple ecosystem, highlighting the power of iCloud, macOS, and other interconnected services. It's likely that many first-time users will appreciate this sheet, as it explains how to get started with Apple services and sync your devices.

Why it matters: For the first-time user, the documentation is a reassurance that help is at hand. Apple's quick start guide is an excellent tool for those who are setting up their first MacBook. It helps you feel confident about starting the setup process and navigating your new device.

5. Apple Stickers

Yes, the iconic Apple stickers are back. Tucked into the manual envelope, you'll find a couple of glossy Apple logo stickers. Whether you choose to stick them on your laptop, water bottle, or favorite notebook, these stickers have become a fun and symbolic part of the Apple experience.

Why it matters: While seemingly small and playful, these stickers represent the sense of belonging to the Apple community. For many, they serve as a personal touch, giving the unboxing experience an extra element of fun and individuality.

6. The Recyclable Packaging

Last but not least, the MacBook Air M4 comes in eco-friendly packaging. Apple has been committed to reducing its environmental impact, and their packaging reflects that effort. The box is made from 100% recycled wood fiber, and the plastics used are minimized as much as possible.

Why it matters: For the eco-conscious first-time user, this is an important step. Knowing that Apple has taken strides to reduce waste and use sustainable materials can make the experience feel even better. It's an added bonus that aligns with Apple's commitment to environmental responsibility.

The Unboxing Experience: A Sense of Anticipation and Excitement

As you lift each item from the box, there's an unmistakable sense of anticipation. The process of unboxing your new MacBook Air M4 isn't just about getting a new piece of tech—it's an experience that sets the tone for your time with the device. Everything from the packaging to the attention to detail in the accessories reinforces the feeling that you're getting something special.

Why it matters: The unboxing experience is the first chapter in your journey with the MacBook Air M4. It's an exciting moment that brings you closer to discovering all the possibilities your new device holds. Each item has been thoughtfully included to ensure that you not only get a device that works well but also enjoy a seamless transition into the Apple ecosystem.

With everything laid out in front of you, it's time to start setting up. But before you dive into the setup process, take a moment to appreciate the experience—because this is just the beginning of what will likely be a long, fruitful relationship with your MacBook Air M4.

Setting Up Your MacBook Air M4 for the First Time

Congratulations on unboxing your brand-new MacBook Air M4! This is the moment you've been waiting for. Whether you're upgrading from a previous MacBook or joining the Apple family for the first time, getting your MacBook Air M4 up and running is a breeze. I'll guide you step by step through the setup process, so you can start enjoying your new device right away.

1. Powering On Your MacBook Air M4

The first step is simple—turn on your MacBook Air M4. To do this, just press the power button located at the top right corner of the keyboard. It's a small, circular button that doubles as the Touch ID sensor. As soon as you press it, you'll see the Apple logo appear on your screen, and your MacBook will start up. This should take just a few seconds, and you'll hear a gentle chime letting you know that everything is working fine.

When you first turn on the MacBook, it'll guide you through the rest of the setup process with on-screen prompts. You'll see a welcoming message, like "Hello" in different languages, which means your Mac is ready to get started.

2. Selecting Your Language and Region

After your MacBook powers up, you'll be prompted to select your language and region. Here's how you can do it:

- **Language**: The first prompt will ask you to choose a language. The options available depend on where you are in the world. If you're in an English-speaking country, English will be the default option, but if you're in a different country or region, other languages will appear as well. Simply click on your preferred language and hit "Continue."

- **Region**: Next, you'll need to select your region or country. This helps macOS tailor your experience, including formatting your time, dates, and currency. It's also important for regional content and services. Select the country or region where you live, and click "Continue."

Don't worry if you accidentally select the wrong language or region at this stage; you can change it later in the System Preferences.

3. Connecting to Wi-Fi

Now it's time to connect to Wi-Fi. Your MacBook Air M4 needs an internet connection to complete the setup process and download the latest updates. Here's how to do it:

- On the next screen, you'll see a list of available Wi-Fi networks. Simply click on your home network from the list.

- If your network is password-protected (and it most likely is), a password prompt will appear. Type in your Wi-Fi password carefully. If you don't remember your password, you might need to check your router or ask someone who knows it.

- Once you've entered your password correctly, hit "Join" or "Connect," and your MacBook will establish a connection.

If you don't have Wi-Fi available or you prefer to connect using an Ethernet cable, there's usually an adapter (sold separately) that you can use to make the connection. However, Wi-Fi is the easiest and most convenient option.

If you're not sure which Wi-Fi network to select, check with someone around you or consult your router settings to ensure you're connecting to the right one.

4. Signing In with Your Apple ID

This is the part where you'll be introduced to one of the best features of the Apple ecosystem: your Apple ID. If you already have an Apple ID (from your iPhone, iPad, or previous Mac), signing in is easy. If not, don't worry—it's quick to create a new one.

- **Sign in with an existing Apple ID**: If you already have an Apple ID, enter your email address and password. If you've set up two-factor authentication, you might receive a prompt to verify your identity via another Apple device or your phone number.

- **Create a new Apple ID**: If you're new to Apple or just need a new ID, click on "Create a Free Apple ID" and follow the instructions to set one up. You'll need to provide some personal information like your name, date of birth, and a valid email address. You'll also be asked to create a password. Make sure your password is something secure, and be sure to write it down somewhere safe.

Once you've logged in or created your Apple ID, your MacBook will automatically start syncing your Apple services, like iCloud, Apple Music,

App Store purchases, and more. If you already use iCloud on your other Apple devices, your photos, contacts, and documents will sync to your MacBook seamlessly.

5. Setting Up Touch ID

The MacBook Air M4 comes with the convenience of Touch ID, allowing you to unlock your MacBook and make purchases with just your fingerprint. Setting this up is quick and easy:

- After signing in with your Apple ID, the next prompt will ask you to set up Touch ID. Place your finger on the power button (located at the top right of your keyboard), and the MacBook will prompt you to lift and rest your finger several times to capture your fingerprint.

- Follow the on-screen instructions, and once you've completed the process, you'll be able to use Touch ID for a variety of tasks, such as logging in, making purchases in the App Store, or authorizing system changes.

This step adds an extra layer of convenience and security to your MacBook, and it's one of the standout features of the M4 model.

6. Agreeing to Terms and Conditions

Next, you'll be asked to review and accept Apple's terms and conditions. While it's not the most exciting part of the setup, it's important that you go through this step. Simply click "Agree" after reading the terms. If you don't want to read the full text, you can scroll to the bottom and accept the terms.

You can also revisit this agreement later under System Preferences > Apple ID.

7. Setting Up iCloud and Apple Services

Once your Apple ID is verified, your MacBook Air M4 will prompt you to enable iCloud and other Apple services. Here's a quick rundown of what these services do:

- **iCloud**: Syncs your photos, documents, calendar, contacts, and other data across all your Apple devices. This ensures you never lose important data and always have access to the latest information.

- **Find My Mac**: This feature is useful if your MacBook ever gets lost or stolen. Enabling "Find My" allows you to track your device's location and remotely lock or erase it if necessary.

- **iCloud Drive**: If you choose to enable this, your documents and files will automatically be backed up to iCloud, making them accessible from any device connected to your Apple ID.

8. Choosing Privacy Settings

Apple is known for its strong privacy protections, and this setup step allows you to control how your data is used. You'll be presented with options to enable location services (for apps that need it, like Maps), analytics (which helps Apple improve its services), and more. Choose the settings that best fit your preferences, but don't worry—Apple will always prioritize your privacy.

9. Finalizing Setup

Once you've completed all the steps above, your MacBook Air M4 will take a few minutes to finalize your settings and apply everything you've selected. You might see a progress bar as the system prepares everything.

Once the setup is complete, you'll be taken to the macOS desktop. Congratulations—you're ready to use your new MacBook!

10. Time to Explore!

Now that your MacBook Air M4 is set up, you can start exploring the MacOS interface, download apps from the Mac App Store, and customize your settings further. You'll find that the MacBook is not only beautiful but also incredibly easy to use, whether you're using it for work, school, or entertainment.

Feel free to go back and tweak your settings or explore new features at any time. The macOS ecosystem is intuitive, and there's a whole world of functionality just waiting to be discovered!

First Impressions: Build Quality, Design, and Display

The moment you lay eyes on the MacBook Air M4, it's clear that Apple has once again set the bar for laptop design. The first impression of the MacBook Air M4 is nothing short of breathtaking. As you slide it out of the box, the slim, elegant profile feels instantly sleek and premium, a testament to Apple's continued commitment to creating beautifully crafted devices. You can't help but run your fingers along the smooth, cold aluminum surface, appreciating the high-quality finish. It feels like you're holding something truly special, something that has been meticulously engineered.

The **build quality** is impeccable, as expected from Apple. The aluminum body, which has been a signature of Apple's laptop lineup for years, is robust yet surprisingly light. At just 2.7 pounds (1.24 kg), this MacBook Air M4 is incredibly portable, allowing you to carry it in a backpack or tote bag with ease. It's the kind of device you don't mind lugging around all day, whether you're heading to the office, a coffee shop, or the couch for some leisurely browsing. Apple's choice of aluminum isn't just about aesthetics; it's about durability. This MacBook Air feels solid, reassuringly sturdy, and ready to endure everyday wear and tear without compromising its sophisticated look.

Now, let's talk about the **design**. One of the most striking features of the MacBook Air M4 is the **new Sky Blue color option**. The color is subtle yet vibrant, and when you see it in person, you'll immediately notice how it exudes a refined, calm vibe. It's not too flashy, but it definitely stands out. Apple's design team has worked hard to ensure that this color isn't just a trendy choice—it's a timeless addition to the MacBook lineup, offering something fresh while staying true to the MacBook's elegant roots.

Even though the design of the M4 shares many similarities with the previous MacBook Airs, such as the same thin profile and minimalistic lines, the M4 does feel like a refinement. Apple has shaved off a few millimeters in thickness, making the MacBook Air M4 even more compact and portable without sacrificing performance. The wedge shape, which tapers from back to front, feels effortlessly modern, giving the device an air of sophistication without being overly bulky or heavy. The edges are neatly rounded, providing a comfortable grip when you hold the device in your hands, and the keyboard and trackpad sit flush with the rest of the body, contributing to its sleek and seamless look.

Speaking of the **keyboard**—Apple has upgraded the typing experience in this model. The scissor-switch mechanism under each key provides a responsive and comfortable typing feel. The keys feel solid yet soft, making typing for long periods an enjoyable experience. Whether you're writing emails, working on a report, or simply chatting with friends, you'll find that the keyboard on the M4 is more than up to the task. The backlighting, which you'll notice as soon as you open the lid, adds to the experience, providing a gentle glow that's both functional and aesthetically pleasing.

Now, let's dive into the **display**—arguably the most significant upgrade in terms of visual experience. The MacBook Air M4 features a stunning **13.6-inch Liquid Retina display** with True Tone technology. The first time you power it on, the screen practically pops to life. The colors are rich and vibrant, with deep blacks and bright whites, making everything from streaming videos to working on creative projects a visual treat. Whether you're watching a movie, editing photos, or simply browsing the web, the display offers clarity and sharpness that feels like it's pulling you into whatever you're doing. The **P3 wide color gamut** ensures that images appear true to life, with a broad range of colors that are accurate and visually appealing.

The **brightness** is another standout feature. At 400 nits, the MacBook Air M4's display is bright enough to use comfortably in a variety of lighting conditions, whether you're in a dimly lit room or sitting by the window with sunlight streaming in. It's a nice touch, especially for those who often work outdoors or in bright environments. The **True Tone** technology, which adjusts the color temperature of the screen to match the ambient light around you, ensures that the display feels natural to your eyes no matter where you are.

One feature that will immediately catch your attention is the **reduced bezels**. Apple has managed to shrink the bezels around the display, giving the M4 a more modern look. This makes the display feel more immersive, as though the screen takes up more of the space and you're left with less interruption from the device's frame. Watching movies or working on creative tasks feels like a more engaging experience because the screen feels more expansive, yet the overall form factor of the device remains incredibly compact.

In terms of **performance**—yes, we'll get into that in more detail later—but from a visual perspective, the M4 chip delivers smooth and snappy performance on the display. Whether you're scrolling through webpages, editing photos in Lightroom, or moving between multiple apps, everything is fluid and responsive. The display doesn't just look good—it's optimized for the demanding needs of users, ensuring that high-performance tasks like video editing or gaming feel comfortable.

Overall, the first impressions of the MacBook Air M4, from its luxurious feel in your hands to the stunning clarity of its display, will leave you in awe. It's a device that blends beauty with functionality, allowing you to enjoy a visually rich experience while offering the power you need to get things done. Whether you're a professional, a student, or someone who just loves top-tier tech, the MacBook Air M4 doesn't just look the part—it *feels* like a step into the future of laptops.

CHAPTER 2: UNDERSTANDING THE HARDWARE

A Closer Look at the MacBook Air M4's Design

The **MacBook Air M4** is more than just a functional device – it's a blend of elegance, cutting-edge technology, and user-centric design that stands out in the crowded world of ultrabooks. Apple has always been known for creating beautifully designed products, but with the introduction of the M4 chip, the MacBook Air takes design to a new level. In this section, we'll take an in-depth look at the MacBook Air M4's physical design, focusing on the color, screen size, weight, and thickness, and compare it to its predecessors to help you understand why this model is a game-changer for Apple.

A Fresh New Color: Sky Blue

One of the first things you'll notice when unboxing the MacBook Air M4 is its stunning new **Sky Blue color**. It's a refreshing, vibrant shade that feels both modern and professional. Apple has taken a step beyond the standard silver and space gray options, offering this sleek new tone that's both visually appealing and calming. This color is subtle yet distinct, not overpowering, but still different enough to set the MacBook Air M4 apart from previous models.

Unlike the traditional metallic finishes found in earlier MacBook models, the **Sky Blue** version offers a smoother, more satin-like finish. It catches the light just right, adding an extra layer of elegance to the device. Whether you're holding it in your hands or setting it on a desk, the reflective nature of the aluminum body draws attention, but in a sophisticated and understated way. It's perfect for anyone looking for a laptop that feels fresh without being overly flashy.

Screen Size: Big Display in a Compact Frame

The MacBook Air M4 boasts a **13.6-inch Retina display**, making it a great choice for users who need a laptop that balances screen real estate with portability. Apple's **Liquid Retina** display technology enhances the visual experience by offering sharp, vibrant colors and impressive clarity. This screen size provides ample space for multitasking, viewing images, editing documents, or watching videos, yet it doesn't overwhelm the user, which is a big improvement over older models that had a slightly smaller display.

The bezels around the screen have been further slimmed down compared to previous generations, making the display feel even larger than it actually is. The **True Tone** technology adjusts the white balance to match the surrounding light, ensuring that your eyes don't strain, whether you're working in bright office light or in a dim room. The screen also features an impressive **P3 wide color gamut**, offering more lifelike colors, which is especially great for those working with creative applications like photo and video editing.

In comparison, older MacBook Air models had a 13.3-inch display with thicker bezels. Although the difference may seem small on paper, the new design provides an immersive viewing experience that's hard to miss when you first lay eyes on the MacBook Air M4.

Weight: Light as Air

One of the hallmarks of the MacBook Air series has always been its featherlight design. The **MacBook Air M4** continues this tradition, weighing in at just **2.7 pounds (1.24 kg)**. This makes it incredibly easy to carry around, whether you're commuting to work, moving between classrooms, or just moving from room to room in your home. The portability is one of the key reasons many users, particularly students and professionals, opt for the MacBook Air.

Even though it's incredibly light, this version doesn't compromise on durability. Apple's **aluminum unibody** construction ensures that it feels solid and sturdy despite its lightweight nature. When you hold it, you won't experience any flex or give, which is a common issue with other lightweight laptops. It's the perfect balance of portability and robustness, making it ideal for on-the-go use.

For comparison, earlier models of the MacBook Air were slightly lighter, but the difference is negligible when considering the **power** and **performance** the M4 offers. The reduced weight is achieved without sacrificing any of the structural integrity that's typical of Apple's designs.

Thickness: Ultra-Thin but Powerful

The MacBook Air M4 is **thinner than ever**, measuring just **0.44 inches (1.13 cm)** at its thickest point. This makes it one of the thinnest laptops on the market, ensuring it slides easily into a backpack or briefcase without taking up much space. The thin profile is a hallmark of the MacBook Air family, and it remains one of the standout features for users who prioritize portability.

In comparison to older MacBook Air models, the M4 is even slimmer, with the wedge shape design that tapers down from the back to the front being more refined. The thinner body makes it easier to carry around, yet it manages to pack in a **larger battery** that offers long-lasting power. Apple has clearly focused on improving the efficiency of its internal components, allowing for an ultra-thin profile without sacrificing battery life or performance.

This thinness also has practical implications for users who need to work from various locations or transport their device frequently. The slim profile allows for maximum flexibility when working in tight spaces, like on a cramped plane seat or at a small coffee shop table.

How It Feels to Hold: Comfortable and Secure

Holding the MacBook Air M4 in your hands feels remarkably comfortable. Apple's **rounded corners** and **smooth finish** allow the laptop to rest naturally in your palms, whether you're carrying it or typing on it. The device is well-balanced, meaning that even though it's light, it doesn't feel flimsy or prone to tipping over when placed on a surface.

The material itself is a joy to touch. The **aluminum finish** provides a premium feel that sets it apart from plastic-bodied competitors. The **matte surface** is smooth but not slippery, so users can comfortably grip it without worrying about it slipping from their hands. The **edge-to-edge design** also ensures that there are no sharp corners digging into your wrists while typing, making long sessions of work or play much more comfortable.

When you compare the feel of the MacBook Air M4 to older models, you'll notice that this new version feels more **solid** and **premium**. The refined edges and smooth surface finish make it comfortable to hold or use in your lap without feeling uncomfortable, something that could be an issue with previous generations of MacBook Airs.

Benefits for Daily Use: A Perfect Blend of Style and Function

The design of the MacBook Air M4 isn't just about aesthetics; it's about enhancing the user experience. The **Sky Blue color** and slim profile make it a visually pleasing device that stands out, while its lightweight and ultra-thin form factor make it perfect for users who are constantly on the go. Whether you're attending meetings, working from a coffee shop, or carrying it in your backpack, the MacBook Air M4's design ensures it won't weigh you down.

Thanks to its compact size and ultra-portable nature, you can take it anywhere. The larger screen and thinner bezels offer a more immersive display without compromising portability. You can easily pull it out in a crowded coffee shop, on a plane, or in a meeting room and feel confident that you're carrying a device that reflects both style and performance.

The combination of the **M4 chip**, **superior build quality**, and **enhanced battery life** also means that this laptop is not just a pretty face – it's a productivity powerhouse. Whether you're working on presentations, editing photos, or simply browsing the web, the MacBook Air M4 is designed to perform at its best while keeping you comfortable and productive.

The M4 Chip: Power, Efficiency, and Performance

The **M4 chip** is the beating heart of the new MacBook Air M4, and it's here to revolutionize the way you use your device. It's not just a new processor; it's the next generation of Apple's custom silicon, designed to deliver exceptional performance while maintaining the energy efficiency that has become synonymous with the MacBook Air. Let's break down what makes the M4 chip so special and how it enhances your experience with the MacBook Air M4.

What is the M4 Chip?

At the core of the MacBook Air M4 is Apple's **M4 chip**, a powerful system-on-a-chip (SoC) that integrates multiple functions—CPU, GPU, neural engine, and more—into a single piece of silicon. This chip is designed not just to handle your daily tasks, but to deliver outstanding performance for demanding applications, all while managing power efficiently.

Think of it like the engine of a high-performance car. Just like how a car's engine determines its speed and fuel efficiency, the M4 chip dictates how fast your MacBook Air runs, how well it handles tasks, and how long its battery lasts.

The Role of the M4 Chip in Performance

The M4 chip is packed with technology that makes the MacBook Air M4 a powerhouse for both **everyday users** and those who demand more from their machines. Here's a breakdown of how the M4 chip improves performance:

1. A New Level of Speed with the CPU

The **central processing unit (CPU)** is the brain of the MacBook Air, responsible for executing most of the tasks you ask it to perform. With the M4 chip, Apple has taken CPU performance to the next level. The M4 features an **8-core CPU**, which consists of high-performance cores and high-efficiency cores.

- **High-Performance Cores**: These are designed to handle demanding tasks, like video editing, gaming, or running multiple applications simultaneously. They're fast and powerful, ensuring that even the most demanding software runs smoothly.

- **High-Efficiency Cores**: These cores are designed for lighter tasks, like web browsing, word processing, or watching videos. They use less power, helping to extend battery life without sacrificing performance for everyday tasks.

This combination of performance and efficiency makes the M4 chip a perfect fit for the MacBook Air, which is known for being a lightweight, portable laptop. Whether you're just checking your emails or running a complex photo-editing project, the M4 chip ensures that you experience quick and seamless performance.

2. Graphics Power with the GPU

While the CPU is responsible for general processing, the **graphics processing unit (GPU)** handles tasks that require visual rendering, like gaming, 3D modeling, and video editing. The M4 chip comes with an **integrated GPU** that is far superior to previous Intel-based MacBook Airs, offering **up to 10 cores of GPU power**.

For **casual users**, the GPU will handle tasks like watching HD movies or browsing social media smoothly, with rich graphics and high-quality video playback. But for **creative professionals**—such as video editors, graphic designers, or anyone working with visually intensive tasks—the M4's GPU offers enhanced performance. Editing 4K videos or rendering complex 3D models on the MacBook Air M4 becomes a breeze, without the need for an external GPU.

3. Neural Engine for Smart Features

Apple's **Neural Engine** is another key element of the M4 chip, and it's built to process machine learning tasks. Whether it's recognizing faces in your photos, improving your app recommendations, or enhancing the performance of intelligent applications like Siri or voice dictation, the Neural Engine makes it all happen seamlessly.

- **For casual users**, this means smarter features like better facial recognition in FaceTime, more accurate suggestions from Siri, and faster voice-to-text capabilities.

- **For power users** who work with AI-based applications or machine learning models, the Neural Engine offers speed and efficiency improvements that can make complex tasks much quicker and more responsive.

4. Energy Efficiency: The Key to Long Battery Life

One of the most impressive aspects of the M4 chip is its **energy efficiency**. Unlike traditional Intel chips, the M4 is optimized for **low-power consumption**, thanks to its ARM architecture. This allows the MacBook Air M4 to deliver high performance without sacrificing battery life.

In fact, the M4 chip is designed to consume significantly less power than older Intel processors, which translates to longer battery life. Apple promises up to **18 hours** of video playback and up to **15 hours of web browsing** on a single charge—something users of previous MacBook Air models would never have imagined possible.

Whether you're working on the go, watching movies, or just using your MacBook Air for light tasks, the M4 chip ensures that the battery will last longer, keeping you productive without needing to charge frequently.

Benefits for Casual Users

For those who use their MacBook Air for everyday tasks—browsing the web, checking emails, watching videos, or using office applications—the M4 chip makes these activities feel faster and more fluid. With its **high-efficiency cores**, the chip ensures that these tasks are done with minimal power consumption, which is why users can expect a laptop that lasts longer between charges.

Furthermore, macOS is optimized to take full advantage of the M4 chip's capabilities, so even the most basic tasks feel faster and more responsive. Pages load quicker in Safari, apps launch almost instantly, and even multitasking is a breeze. The M4 chip provides an experience that feels smooth and effortless, no matter what you're doing.

Benefits for Demanding Tasks

For **power users** or those who push their MacBook Air M4 to the limit with heavy tasks like **photo editing**, **video editing**, **coding**, or **design work**, the M4 chip excels.

- **Photo editing** in apps like Adobe Photoshop or Lightroom will feel lightning-fast, with quicker rendering times and smooth handling of high-resolution images.

- **Video editing** in Final Cut Pro or Adobe Premiere Pro will be much more responsive, allowing you to scrub through footage, add effects, and render videos in a fraction of the time compared to older MacBook Air models.

- **Gaming** performance is also noticeably improved, as the M4's powerful GPU ensures smoother graphics and faster frame rates for casual games or even more graphics-intensive titles.

The combination of the **M4 chip's CPU and GPU** means that no matter how demanding the task, your MacBook Air will rise to the occasion—without breaking a sweat.

A Game Changer for Multitasking

Thanks to the M4 chip's combination of high-performance cores, energy-efficient cores, and integrated GPU, the MacBook Air M4 handles multitasking like never before. You can run multiple apps, keep several browser tabs open, and have video calls all at once, without experiencing lag or slowdowns.

Whether you're editing a document, replying to emails, and streaming a video at the same time, the M4 chip ensures you can juggle multiple tasks without compromise. This is a game-changer for users who need to stay productive while managing multiple projects simultaneously.

Battery Life and Power Management Tips

One of the standout features of the MacBook Air M4 is its remarkable battery life. Thanks to the efficiency of the new M4 chip, you can expect your device to handle long hours of use without needing a charge, which is perfect for students, professionals, or anyone on the go. But even with such impressive battery performance, there are always ways to extend the longevity of your MacBook Air M4's battery, ensuring it stays in top shape for years to come.

Here are some practical tips for maximizing battery life and power management on your MacBook Air M4.

1. Enable Low Power Mode

Low Power Mode is a feature built into macOS that helps extend your battery life when you're running low on power. By reducing system performance, dimming the screen, and lowering energy usage in the background, your MacBook Air M4 can go much longer without needing a recharge.

To turn on **Low Power Mode**:

1. **Click on the Apple logo** in the top-left corner of your screen.

2. Select **System Preferences**.

3. Go to **Battery**.

4. Check the box next to **Low Power Mode**.

When you're traveling or working away from a charger, Low Power Mode is a great way to stretch your battery even further. Keep in mind, though, that while it improves battery life, it can reduce the MacBook's processing power, so it's best used for basic tasks like reading, browsing, or writing.

2. Battery Optimization with macOS Features

The **Battery Health Management** feature in macOS is designed to improve the long-term health of your MacBook's battery by reducing the rate at which it chemically ages. This feature limits the maximum charge when it detects that a full charge isn't necessary for your current usage patterns, which can help prevent battery wear over time.

To enable **Battery Health Management**:

1. Open **System Preferences**.

2. Select **Battery**.

3. Choose **Battery Health** and ensure that the **Battery Health Management** box is checked.

Battery Health Management helps you keep your battery in peak condition, and you'll likely see less deterioration in its ability to hold charge over the years, extending the overall lifespan of your device.

3. Adjusting Screen Brightness

One of the biggest drains on your MacBook's battery is the **screen brightness**. The brighter your screen, the more energy it uses, so if you're trying to preserve battery life, consider adjusting the brightness to a lower level.

Here's how to adjust screen brightness:

- Use the **F1** and **F2 keys** to decrease and increase the brightness, respectively.

- Or, go to **System Preferences** > **Displays** and adjust the brightness slider.

Auto-Brightness is another great feature that helps you save energy. With Auto-Brightness, your MacBook will automatically adjust the screen brightness based on the surrounding lighting conditions, ensuring you're not using more energy than necessary.

To enable Auto-Brightness:

1. Go to **System Preferences** > **Displays**.

2. Check the option for **Automatically adjust brightness**.

4. Close Unnecessary Apps and Background Processes

Every app or process running on your MacBook uses up battery power, even if you're not actively using it. To maximize battery life, be mindful of the programs you leave running in the background.

To close apps and processes:

1. Open **Activity Monitor** (you can find it by searching Spotlight).

2. Look for any processes using excessive CPU or energy and **quit** them if they're unnecessary.

Additionally, don't forget to **quit apps** that you're not actively using. You can either close them from the **Dock** or use **Cmd + Q** to quit them fully.

5. Disable Wi-Fi and Bluetooth When Not in Use

Wi-Fi and Bluetooth are great for connecting to the internet, your wireless devices, and external accessories, but when you're not using them, they can drain your battery by constantly searching for networks and devices.

To conserve power:

- **Turn off Wi-Fi** when you're not using it by clicking on the Wi-Fi icon in the top-right corner and selecting **Turn Wi-Fi Off**.

- Similarly, **turn off Bluetooth** by clicking the Bluetooth icon and selecting **Turn Bluetooth Off** if you don't need to connect to any Bluetooth devices.

6. Manage Your Energy Settings

macOS provides energy-saving settings that can help you manage when and how your MacBook Air M4 uses power. To ensure your MacBook isn't using unnecessary energy when it's idle, adjust these settings.

Here's how to adjust energy preferences:

1. Open **System Preferences**.

2. Go to **Battery**.

3. Choose **Energy Saver** settings, and you can select options like turning off hard disk sleep, dimming the display when inactive, and allowing your MacBook to sleep when idle for a set amount of time.

Setting your Mac to automatically sleep after a period of inactivity is particularly useful if you tend to leave your MacBook on for long periods. This will ensure that it's not draining power while you're away.

7. Turn Off Unused Visual Effects

macOS includes some neat visual effects, but these effects can also consume more battery power, especially when you're working on demanding tasks. While they make your MacBook look beautiful, they aren't always necessary.

To minimize these effects:

1. Go to **System Preferences** > **Accessibility**.

2. Under the **Display** section, check the box for **Reduce motion** and **Reduce transparency**.

These small adjustments can reduce the graphical load on your MacBook, helping you extend battery life without sacrificing too much of the user experience.

8. Avoid Extreme Temperatures

MacBook batteries, like all lithium-ion batteries, do not perform well in extreme temperatures. Using your MacBook in environments that are too hot or too cold can shorten battery life and reduce its overall lifespan.

To preserve battery health:

- Keep your MacBook Air M4 in a room temperature environment (between 50°F and 95°F or 10°C and 35°C).

- Avoid leaving your MacBook in direct sunlight or in a car on a hot day.

Additionally, **charging in a cool environment** is better for battery health, so ensure you're not charging your MacBook on a soft surface like a bed or pillow, which can trap heat.

9. Update macOS Regularly

Sometimes, Apple releases updates that include performance improvements and optimizations, including fixes that help extend battery life. Be sure to regularly check for macOS updates to take advantage of any optimizations Apple has made.

To check for updates:

1. Click the **Apple logo** in the top-left corner.

2. Select **System Preferences** > **Software Update**.

3. If there's an update available, click **Update Now**.

Keeping your MacBook up-to-date ensures it's running as efficiently as possible, which can help improve battery performance.

10. Monitor Battery Usage

macOS provides you with detailed insights into how your battery is being used, so you can better understand which apps and processes are draining your battery.

To check your battery usage:

1. Click the **battery icon** in the top-right corner.

2. From the drop-down, you'll see **Battery Usage** and which apps are consuming the most power.

By being mindful of your battery usage and making adjustments based on these insights, you can prioritize what's most important and conserve power for the tasks that matter most.

Webcam and Audio Performance

When it comes to staying connected with friends, family, colleagues, or classmates, video calls have become a cornerstone of modern communication. Whether you're working remotely, attending virtual classes, or catching up with loved ones, the quality of your webcam and audio is crucial. The **MacBook Air M4** takes these experiences to the next level with its newly upgraded **12MP Center Stage webcam** and advanced **audio capabilities**, ensuring that every video call and multimedia experience is crystal clear and immersive. Let's dive into how these features enhance your everyday digital interactions and why they stand out in the crowded market of laptops.

The 12MP Center Stage Webcam: A Game-Changer for Video Calls

In previous MacBook Air models, the webcam was a relatively basic 720p camera that did its job but left much to be desired when it came to high-quality video calls. Enter the **12MP Center Stage webcam** in the MacBook Air M4—a significant leap forward in terms of both resolution and functionality. This camera is not just about sharp, high-definition images; it's about creating an experience that feels natural, engaging, and professional.

High-Quality Resolution and Clearer Images

First off, the **12MP resolution** offers an incredible level of clarity, making every detail sharp and vibrant. Whether you're attending a Zoom meeting, FaceTiming with family, or recording a vlog, the **MacBook Air M4's webcam** ensures that you look your best. The upgrade from the previous 720p camera is noticeable, with smoother and more vibrant colors, giving you an image quality that matches modern expectations.

What makes this webcam even more impressive is its **Center Stage** feature. This innovative technology uses the power of the M4 chip's processing capabilities to keep you in frame during a video call, even if you move around. Unlike traditional webcams that remain static, **Center Stage** automatically adjusts the camera's framing to follow you, making it ideal for situations where you're moving, such as giving a presentation, walking around during a meeting, or even trying to juggle multiple tasks on screen.

Center Stage: Intelligent Tracking for Seamless Interaction

The **Center Stage** feature relies on machine learning and the camera's wide field of view to dynamically adjust the framing. It can recognize your movements and, if others are in the frame, automatically zoom in and out to keep everyone properly centered. For example, during a group video call, if someone else enters the frame or you lean in for a closer view, the camera adjusts to ensure everyone is seen clearly. This level of intelligent adjustment ensures that the focus is always where it needs to be, without the need for manual intervention. It's a game-changer for personal and professional meetings alike, as it makes your video calls feel much more interactive and natural.

Low-Light Performance

The 12MP Center Stage webcam is also designed to perform exceptionally well in low-light conditions. Thanks to the improved sensor and Apple's advanced image processing, you won't need to worry about looking washed out or overly dark in dimly lit rooms. The camera automatically enhances lighting, making sure your face is well-lit even if you're in a dimly lit space, reducing the need for additional lighting equipment for your video calls.

Audio Performance: Immersive Sound for Video Calls and Entertainment

While a high-quality webcam is essential, audio quality is equally important for an enjoyable video calling and multimedia experience. The **MacBook Air M4** delivers an exceptional audio experience, thanks to its enhanced speaker system and improved microphone setup.

High-Fidelity Stereo Speakers

Apple has designed the MacBook Air M4 with **stereo speakers** that produce **richer, fuller sound**. Whether you're watching a movie, listening to music, or participating in a video call, the sound is clear and balanced. The speakers are positioned to project sound in an immersive way, offering deeper bass and higher clarity compared to previous MacBook Air models. Even in a crowded room, the speakers manage to produce sound that is loud enough to fill the space without distortion, making it perfect for listening to podcasts, streaming content, or engaging in virtual meetings.

Wide Stereo Sound for Enhanced Audio Quality

The **wide stereo sound** feature is especially helpful when you're attending virtual meetings or watching content on the MacBook Air M4. Unlike most laptops that offer a somewhat narrow sound experience, the MacBook Air M4 provides audio that spreads out across a wider range, ensuring that every word, note, and sound is heard with clarity. The inclusion of **spatial audio** technology, supported by the M4 chip, enhances the audio experience further by creating a surround-sound effect that makes it feel like you're in the middle of the action.

Improved Microphone Array for Crystal-Clear Voice Pickup

The **MacBook Air M4** comes with an advanced **three-microphone array** that picks up your voice with remarkable clarity. This is particularly important for video calls, where clear audio is critical. No more straining to hear soft voices or dealing with muffled sound. Whether you're speaking softly or having a discussion in a noisy environment, the MacBook Air M4's microphones adapt to ensure your voice is heard loud and clear.

The microphones work hand-in-hand with **machine learning algorithms** to filter out background noise and focus on the speaker's voice. Whether you're in a noisy cafe, a bustling office, or a quiet home office, the MacBook Air M4 automatically reduces distractions and enhances the clarity of your voice. This makes it ideal for professional meetings or personal calls where background noise can be an issue.

What Sets It Apart from Previous Models

Compared to earlier MacBook Air models, the webcam and audio system in the M4 is leaps ahead in terms of both performance and usability. The 12MP webcam and Center Stage technology offer a level of interactivity and clarity that wasn't available before, especially with the previous 720p camera. The shift from a static webcam to one that intelligently tracks movements sets the M4 apart from not just previous MacBook models, but many laptops on the market today.

The audio system, too, is an upgrade from previous models. With stereo speakers, high-fidelity sound, and improved microphones, the MacBook Air M4 offers a much more immersive multimedia experience, whether you're listening to music, participating in a video call, or watching your favorite TV show.

Real-Life Benefits

For everyday users, the upgraded webcam and audio system make video calls more enjoyable and productive. **Center Stage** ensures that you're always perfectly framed, no matter how much you move around, creating a more engaging experience for both you and those on the other side of the call. For business professionals, this feature helps make virtual meetings feel more natural and dynamic, eliminating the awkwardness of being off-center during a conversation.

The superior audio system ensures that voice clarity is always at its best, whether you're giving a presentation, collaborating with colleagues, or chatting with family members. The **MacBook Air M4** becomes not just a device for communication but an entertainment hub, thanks to the full-spectrum audio and crystal-clear visuals.

CHAPTER 3: EXPLORING MACOS

Introduction to macOS: Getting Comfortable with the Interface

Welcome to your journey with macOS, the intuitive and beautifully designed operating system that powers your MacBook Air M4. If you're coming from Windows or are new to Apple's ecosystem, it might seem like a whole new world. But don't worry—getting comfortable with macOS is easier than you think, and soon, you'll be navigating your MacBook like a pro.

Let's break down the interface, starting with the essentials that will make you feel right at home: the **desktop**, **Finder**, and **System Preferences**. By the end of this chapter, you'll be able to confidently navigate your MacBook Air M4 and find everything you need with ease.

The Desktop: Your Command Center

When you first power on your MacBook Air M4, you're greeted with the **desktop**, the central workspace where all your apps, files, and folders come to life. It's like the command center for your digital world.

- **The Menu Bar**: The top part of the screen is the **Menu Bar**. This area contains everything you need for quick access to MacBook functions. From left to right, you'll find the **Apple Menu**, which provides access to system preferences, shutdown options, and recent documents. Next is the **App Menu**, which changes based on the app you're using—it's where you can find specific app controls like "Save," "Quit," or "Preferences." On the far-right, you'll find useful icons like Wi-Fi, battery status, time, and the spotlight search.

- **The Dock**: At the bottom of your screen, you'll see the **Dock**—a horizontal row of icons for quick access to your favorite apps, minimized windows, and frequently used folders. You can customize the Dock to suit your needs. If you want to add an app to the Dock, simply drag it from the **Applications** folder and place it there. To remove an app, just drag it out of the Dock—no worries, it won't delete the app, it's just removed from the shortcut.

- **The Desktop Background**: Your desktop is your personal space—it's where your files, folders, and applications live. You can change the **wallpaper** to something that reflects your personality. Right-click anywhere on the desktop, select **Change Desktop Background**, and pick a wallpaper from the options or upload your own. It's a small customization, but it helps make your Mac feel like *your* Mac.

Finder: Your Digital Organizer

One of the most powerful features of macOS is **Finder,** the file management tool that helps you organize everything on your MacBook. Think of Finder as your digital filing cabinet—it's where you store, organize, and search for files, folders, and apps.

- **Opening Finder**: To open Finder, simply click on the **Finder** icon in the Dock (the first icon that looks like a smiling face). You can also use the keyboard shortcut **Command + Space** to bring up **Spotlight Search** and type "Finder."

- **Finder Windows**: When you open Finder, it opens up a **window** where you can see all your files and folders. Think of it as a window into your Mac's storage. By default, Finder opens the **Recents** view, which shows recently accessed files. On the left side of the window, you'll see the **sidebar**, which includes shortcuts to important locations like **Documents**, **Downloads**, and **Applications**.

- **Navigating Finder**: The Finder window is divided into two main sections: the **sidebar** and the **main viewing area**. In the sidebar, you'll find folders, devices, and network locations that you can access quickly. The main area shows the contents of the folder you have selected in the sidebar.

  - You can click on a folder in the sidebar (e.g., **Documents**) to see all its contents in the main area. If you want to open a file, just double-click on it.

  - Finder also lets you organize files by type, date, or name. To sort files, click on the **View** menu at the top of the screen, select **Show View Options**, and choose how you'd like your files to be displayed.

MACBOOK AIR M4 USER GUIDE

- **Using Tags in Finder**: A cool feature of Finder is **Tags**, which allows you to color-code and label your files for easy identification. If you're working on a project and need to find related files quickly, you can tag them by right-clicking the file, selecting **Tags**, and picking a color or creating a custom tag name. Later, you can use the **Tags** section in Finder's sidebar to see all files with that tag.

System Preferences: Your Personal Settings Hub

Now that you've got the hang of navigating your MacBook's desktop and Finder, it's time to explore **System Preferences**—this is where you can customize and tweak your MacBook Air M4 to suit your needs. It's like the control center for all things system-related.

- **Opening System Preferences**: Click the **Apple Menu** in the top-left corner of the screen and select **System Preferences**. Alternatively, you can find **System Preferences** by opening Spotlight and typing it in.

- **Navigating System Preferences**: Inside **System Preferences**, you'll find a grid of icons, each representing different settings for your Mac. Some key areas to check out include:

  - **General**: Customize your desktop appearance, color schemes (light or dark mode), and more.

  - **Desktop & Screen Saver**: Here you can change your desktop background and set a screen saver.

- o **Dock & Menu Bar**: Adjust the size of the Dock, its position (left, bottom, or right), and other options like whether to magnify the Dock icons.

- o **Security & Privacy**: Manage privacy settings for apps, choose which apps have access to your location, contacts, photos, and more. This is a critical area to ensure your MacBook remains secure.

- o **Battery**: Customize energy-saving settings to extend your MacBook's battery life.

- o **Sound**: Here you can control the volume, input/output devices, and even adjust the balance between speakers and headphones.

- **Using the Search Bar**: As you explore the System Preferences, you'll notice a **search bar** at the top right corner. You can type anything here to quickly find specific settings without scrolling through the entire list.

Spotlight Search: Your Search Superpower

macOS includes **Spotlight Search**, a tool that helps you find anything on your Mac quickly. It's like having your own digital assistant to help you locate files, apps, emails, and even information from the web.

- **Opening Spotlight**: Press **Command + Space** to bring up Spotlight, or click the magnifying glass icon in the top-right corner of your screen.

- **How to Use Spotlight**: Once the Spotlight window appears, just start typing what you're looking for. For example, type "Safari" to open the Safari browser, or type "Invoices" to find any document with that name. Spotlight can also search the web, look up definitions, and even do calculations.

Navigating macOS: Additional Tips for Beginners

- **The Control Center**: The **Control Center** is your go-to spot for adjusting common settings like Wi-Fi, Bluetooth, volume, and Do Not Disturb. You can access it by clicking the **Control Center** icon in the menu bar (it looks like two toggles). This is super handy when you need to change settings on the fly.

- **Exposé and Mission Control**: If you've got multiple windows or apps open, **Mission Control** helps you see all of them at a glance. You can swipe up on your trackpad with three or four fingers to activate **Mission Control**. If you want to quickly switch between open apps, swipe left or right on the trackpad with three fingers to move between them.

- **Gestures**: macOS supports a variety of **gestures** that make navigating your MacBook easier. For example, you can **swipe with three fingers** to switch between apps, or **pinch with three fingers** to enter full-screen mode. If you're unsure about which gestures are available, head to **System Preferences > Trackpad** to view all of them.

Navigating macOS: Finder, System Preferences, and More

Welcome to the world of macOS, where everything is designed with simplicity, elegance, and efficiency in mind. If you're new to the MacBook Air M4, navigating macOS might seem a little different from what you're used to, but don't worry! This chapter will walk you through the basics of using macOS in the most intuitive way possible.

We'll dive into **Finder**, your ultimate file management tool, and explore **System Preferences**, the control center for personalizing your MacBook. Plus, we'll sprinkle in some tips and tricks to make using macOS feel like second nature. By the end of this chapter, you'll have a firm grasp on how to navigate macOS smoothly and efficiently.

The Basics of Finder: Your File Management Hub

Think of **Finder** as your MacBook's file manager—it's where all your documents, applications, photos, and other files live. It's not just a place to view your files; it's a powerful tool that helps you organize, search, and access anything on your Mac. Let's break it down.

What is Finder?

Finder is the first thing you'll see when you open your MacBook Air M4. It's always running in the background and is accessible through the **Finder icon** at the far-left side of your Dock (the row of apps at the bottom of the screen). You can also use the **Command + N** shortcut to open a new Finder window.

Basic Features of Finder

When you open Finder, you'll see several essential elements:

1. **Sidebar**: The left column that lets you quickly access common locations like your **Desktop, Documents, Downloads, iCloud Drive**, and external drives. It's customizable, so you can add your most-used folders for easy access.

2. **Toolbar**: At the top of the Finder window, the toolbar lets you navigate between different views of your files. Here, you can search your entire system using **Spotlight** (more on that soon), change your view (icon, list, or column), and sort files.

3. **File Views**: The Finder lets you choose how you view your files. You can display them as icons, in a list, or in columns. To switch between these views, simply click the corresponding icon in the toolbar. The **Column View** is especially useful because it shows you a file's path and allows you to navigate through folders with a simple click.

Working with Files in Finder

Now that you know the basics, let's talk about how to actually manage your files:

- **Creating New Folders**: Right-click anywhere inside a folder and select **New Folder**. You can also use the **Command + Shift + N** shortcut to create a folder instantly.

- **Moving Files**: To move a file, simply drag it to the desired location. You can also copy files by holding down the **Option** key while dragging them.

- **Quick Look**: Want to preview a file without opening it? Select it in Finder and press the **Spacebar**. This will show a quick preview of the file, whether it's a document, image, or video. It's a time-saving feature that comes in handy.

- **Searching with Spotlight**: In the top-right corner of Finder, there's a search bar. You can start typing the name of a file, folder, or app, and Spotlight will instantly filter results. Spotlight also gives you the option to filter by file type, date modified, and more.

System Preferences: Customizing Your MacBook Air M4

Now that you've got Finder down, let's dive into **System Preferences**, the heart of personalizing your Mac. This is where you adjust everything from the way your MacBook looks to how it behaves.

You can access **System Preferences** by clicking on the **Apple logo** in the top-left corner of your screen, then selecting **System Preferences** from the dropdown menu.

Navigating System Preferences

The **System Preferences** window is organized into several categories that you can click to explore further. These categories cover everything from your **display settings** to your **security preferences**.

- **General**: This is where you can adjust the appearance of your Mac. Want a light or dark theme? This is where you control that. You can also adjust the size of your icons in the Dock, as well as choose how your desktop and screensaver look.

- **Desktop & Screen Saver**: If you want to change your wallpaper, add a screensaver, or adjust display settings (like resolution), this is the place to go.

- **Dock & Menu Bar**: Customize your Dock, where all your apps are pinned. You can change the position of the Dock (bottom, left, or right), choose whether to hide it, and even make it auto-hide when you don't need it. The **Menu Bar** lets you personalize the icons at the top of the screen, like volume and Wi-Fi.

- **Mission Control**: Mission Control gives you an overview of all open windows and spaces, making it easier to switch between apps. You can activate it with a swipe-up gesture on the trackpad or by pressing the **F3** key.

Other Important Preferences

Here are a few more System Preferences settings that you should know about:

- **Trackpad**: This is where you adjust how the trackpad behaves, including scrolling, tapping, and gestures. The MacBook Air M4's trackpad supports multi-finger gestures for actions like zooming and switching between desktops.

- **Apple ID**: If you're using iCloud, this is where you can sign in to your Apple account and manage your iCloud settings, including syncing your photos, documents, and more.

- **Security & Privacy**: Here, you can manage your privacy settings, control app permissions, and enable security features like **FileVault** (which encrypts your data to keep it secure) and **Firewall** settings. This is a key area to visit if you're concerned about security.

Tips & Tricks to Navigate macOS Faster

By now, you should have a good understanding of the basics, but let's take it a step further with some tips and tricks that will help you navigate macOS like a pro:

1. **Use Spotlight for Quick Access**: Press **Command + Spacebar** to bring up **Spotlight**, and use it to search for files, apps, and even perform quick calculations or conversions. It's the fastest way to access anything on your MacBook Air M4.

2. **Use Stacks to Stay Organized**: If your Desktop gets cluttered with files, enable **Stacks**. This automatically organizes your files into categories like documents, images, and PDFs, making your desktop

much tidier. To enable Stacks, right-click on the desktop and select **Use Stacks**.

3. **Drag Files Between Apps with Split View**: When working on multiple tasks, use **Split View** to place two apps side by side. You can then drag and drop files from Finder into other applications with ease.

4. **Customize the Touchpad**: Head to **System Preferences > Trackpad**, and you can customize gestures to make navigation even easier. For example, you can set up a three-finger swipe to switch between desktops or launch Mission Control.

5. **Use Hot Corners**: Hot Corners are a neat little feature that lets you activate certain actions (like starting screensavers or showing the desktop) by moving your cursor to a corner of the screen. To set this up, go to **System Preferences > Mission Control > Hot Corners**.

6. **Quickly Hide Windows**: Need to quickly hide a window? Press **Command + H** to hide the active window and clear up your screen without closing anything.

Spotlight Search: The Fastest Way to Find What You Need

One of the most powerful features of macOS, yet often overlooked by new users, is **Spotlight Search**. Think of it as your MacBook's ultimate search engine, but tailored specifically to help you navigate and access everything on your computer with just a few keystrokes. Whether you're looking for a document, an app, an email, or even just a piece of information buried deep in a file, Spotlight is the quickest way to find it.

What is Spotlight Search?

Spotlight Search is a system-wide search tool that allows you to quickly locate files, folders, emails, apps, contacts, calendar events, and even information from the web. By simply pressing a few keys, you can search your entire MacBook for what you need, without having to dig through folders or open multiple apps.

It's like having a superpower for your MacBook—everything you need is at your fingertips in seconds.

How to Access Spotlight Search

Getting started with Spotlight Search is easy:

1. **Shortcut**: Press **Command (⌘) + Spacebar** on your keyboard. This will instantly open Spotlight's search bar at the top-right corner of your screen.

2. **Clicking the Spotlight Icon**: Alternatively, you can click on the magnifying glass icon located in the upper-right corner of your screen (next to the Wi-Fi and battery icons). This will open the Spotlight search bar.

Once the search bar is open, you can begin typing whatever you're looking for. Spotlight will start offering suggestions right away—no need to hit "Enter" unless you want to see more results.

Using Spotlight to Search for Apps

Let's say you're trying to open an app, but you don't want to go searching through the Applications folder or the Launchpad. With Spotlight, it's all about speed.

For example, if you want to open **Safari**, just hit **Command (⌘) + Spacebar** to bring up Spotlight. Then, start typing "Safari"—within seconds, the app will pop up as one of the top suggestions. You can hit **Enter** to launch the app, or simply click on it with your mouse.

Spotlight is smart enough to list apps that you use often near the top, so you don't have to type the full name every time. Let's say you use **Mail** regularly, just typing **"M"** might bring up Mail as a suggestion, and you can hit **Enter** right away.

Finding Files and Documents

Spotlight is not just for apps. It's incredibly useful when you're looking for a file, document, or folder that you might have saved months ago and don't remember exactly where it's located.

Let's say you're working on a project and need a specific file but can't quite remember the name of it. Instead of wasting time searching through your Documents or Downloads folder, open Spotlight and start typing a keyword related to the file. For instance, if you were working on a **resume**, typing

"resume" will show a list of all files containing the word "resume." Spotlight doesn't just search filenames—it can also look inside documents to find any text that matches your search term.

Example:

You've been working on a presentation titled "Marketing Strategy" but can't remember where you saved it. If you type "Marketing Strategy" into Spotlight, it will immediately list all files related to that term, including any documents, images, or PDFs. It even indexes text within files, so you can search for specific phrases or words inside documents without needing to open them.

Searching for Emails and Calendar Events

Spotlight doesn't limit itself to just local files—it can also search through your **Mail** and **Calendar** to bring up relevant emails or events.

For example, let's say you need to find a specific email from a colleague about a **meeting** next Tuesday. You can type something as simple as "meeting" into Spotlight, and it will search through your Mail app to pull up related messages. You can narrow it down further by typing the name of the person or the subject of the email.

Similarly, if you have a **meeting scheduled** in your Calendar, typing the event's name or even just the date into Spotlight will bring it up instantly. This saves you from having to open the Calendar app and search manually.

Searching the Web with Spotlight

What makes Spotlight even more powerful is its ability to **search the web** without opening Safari or any other browser. It can search through sources like **Wikipedia**, **Google**, and even show you relevant results from the **App Store** and **iTunes**.

For instance, if you type in "apple" in Spotlight, it will show you:

- A **Wikipedia article** about the fruit or the tech company

- Relevant **news stories** from the web

- Suggestions for apps related to apples, or even recipes

- Apple-related songs or podcasts from iTunes

Using Spotlight for Calculations and Unit Conversions

One of the often-overlooked features of Spotlight is its ability to handle simple **calculations** and **unit conversions**.

You can use it as a quick calculator by typing expressions like:

- **45 * 12**

- **320 / 4**

- **1000 + 500** Spotlight will instantly give you the result without you needing to open the Calculator app.

Spotlight can also convert units, whether it's currency, distance, or weight. Type something like:

- **10 USD to EUR** (to convert US dollars to euros)

- **10 miles to kilometers** Spotlight will give you the conversion on the spot, making it super convenient for quick calculations.

Using Spotlight to Launch System Preferences

Spotlight also lets you search for specific **system settings** without diving into the System Preferences app. For instance, if you want to adjust the **display settings**, just type "Display" into Spotlight, and you'll be taken directly to the Display settings in System Preferences. This eliminates the need to manually search through the System Preferences panel.

Example:

If you need to adjust the **brightness** or **resolution** of your MacBook's screen, instead of navigating through multiple menus, just type **"Display"** in Spotlight. Click on the result, and you'll be taken straight to the settings.

Refining Your Spotlight Search

As your search results populate, you may notice multiple categories appear, such as Documents, Folders, Contacts, Apps, and more. To refine your search, Spotlight offers **categories** that let you filter through the results.

For instance, if you're looking for a document and don't want to see apps or emails, you can click on the **"Documents"** category to only see relevant results. You can also scroll through the suggestions to find exactly what you need.

If you're a power user, you might want to take things a step further by using **advanced search operators**. For example:

- **Kind:** to specify the type of file (e.g., "Kind: PDF" to find all PDFs)

- **Created:** to find files created within a specific time frame (e.g., "Created: Last week")

- **Name:** to search for a specific file by name (e.g., "Name: Budget")

Practical Examples of Spotlight in Action

Here are a few real-world scenarios where Spotlight can save you time and effort:

- **Finding a specific email**: Instead of going into your Mail app, type "from:John Doe" into Spotlight to bring up all emails from John, instantly narrowing down your search.

- **Accessing a file quickly**: If you need to open a document called "Project Plan" that's buried in a subfolder, type "Project Plan" in Spotlight, and it will appear in seconds, saving you from browsing through folders.

- **Finding a contact**: Want to call or message someone? Just type their name into Spotlight, and you'll see their contact details pop up for you to act on right away.

Pre-installed Apps: What's New and What's Useful

When you first power up your **MacBook Air M4**, one of the first things you'll notice is that it comes with a suite of pre-installed apps that are designed to make your life easier, more organized, and more productive. These apps are fully integrated into macOS, allowing you to do everything from browsing the web to managing your finances. In this section, we'll take a deep dive into the most important pre-installed apps on the MacBook Air M4, explore what's new, and show you exactly how to use them to get the most out of your device.

Whether you're a student, a professional, or someone just looking to stay organized, these apps will quickly become essential to your everyday tasks.

1. Safari: Fast, Secure Browsing

What it is: Safari is Apple's native web browser, designed to be fast, efficient, and privacy-focused. With its clean interface, lightning-fast performance, and deep integration with the macOS ecosystem, Safari is not just a browser—it's a tool that helps you stay productive and secure online.

What's new: In the MacBook Air M4, Safari comes with improved energy efficiency, meaning you can browse for longer without draining your battery. The latest version also features **tab grouping**, which lets you organize your tabs into categories, making it easier to manage multiple web pages at once.

MACBOOK AIR M4 USER GUIDE

How it works: Safari offers a streamlined experience, allowing you to search, navigate, and organize websites with ease. You can open multiple tabs, pin your favorite sites, and even use **Handoff** to continue browsing seamlessly between your MacBook Air M4 and iPhone or iPad.

How it helps:

- **Web browsing**: With built-in tools like **Reader Mode**, Safari helps you eliminate distractions on websites and focus on the content that matters.

- **Password management**: Safari's **AutoFill** feature remembers your passwords and logins for websites, saving you the headache of having to remember every single one.

- **Privacy features**: Safari is known for its privacy-first approach. It includes **Intelligent Tracking Prevention**, which helps block cross-site tracking, and a privacy report that gives you insight into how websites are tracking you.

Practical Example: Imagine you're researching a school project and need to access multiple sources. Safari's **tab grouping** allows you to organize your research into different categories like "Articles," "Videos," and "References." You can easily switch between groups without losing track of what you were doing.

2. Mail: Streamlined Email Management

What it is: Mail is macOS's native email client, and it's designed to work seamlessly with all major email services like Gmail, Yahoo, Outlook, and of

MACBOOK AIR M4 USER GUIDE

course, iCloud. Whether you're managing work emails or personal messages, Mail keeps everything organized.

What's new: The Mail app has been revamped in macOS to include features like **conversation view** (which groups related emails together), **improved search functionality**, and a **smart compose** feature that suggests complete sentences based on your writing style.

How it works: Mail allows you to easily send, receive, and organize your emails. You can create folders, flag important messages, and even schedule emails to be sent at a later time. Its integration with the Apple ecosystem means you can send an email from your MacBook Air M4 and access it on your iPhone later.

How it helps:

- **Productivity**: You can use **Smart Folders** to automatically organize incoming emails by criteria you set, like specific senders or keywords.

- **Search**: The improved search functionality allows you to find exactly what you're looking for in seconds—whether it's an attachment, contact, or message.

- **Security**: Mail also includes **Mail Privacy Protection**, which ensures that the sender cannot track when or where you open their emails.

Practical Example: Let's say you're working on a project with colleagues and need to keep track of all communications related to it. You can create a **Smart Folder** that automatically collects all emails with a specific keyword like "Project Name" or from certain team members. This way, all your emails are in one place, making it easier to find information.

3. Photos: Organize, Edit, and Share Your Memories

What it is: Photos is your digital photo album, but with a twist. It not only organizes your photos and videos but also includes powerful editing tools and seamless integration with iCloud, so your memories are always with you, no matter what device you're using.

What's new: The MacBook Air M4 comes with **photo editing improvements**, including new tools like **Auto Enhance** and advanced color adjustment features. There's also improved **Live Photos** functionality, allowing you to edit and create fun, interactive experiences from your still images.

How it works: Photos automatically organizes your pictures into albums by year, location, and even people. It also allows you to create custom albums, edit photos with a full suite of tools, and share your favorite memories with friends and family via social media or iCloud links.

How it helps:

- **Organization**: **Smart Albums** can automatically sort your photos based on criteria like location, date, and even the type of photo.

- **Editing**: You don't need third-party apps for basic photo edits. The Photos app lets you adjust exposure, brightness, contrast, and even crop photos in an intuitive, easy-to-use interface.

- **Sharing**: With iCloud integration, you can **sync your entire photo library** across all your Apple devices, so you never have to worry about losing your precious memories.

Practical Example: Suppose you just got back from a vacation, and you have hundreds of photos on your MacBook Air M4. You can use the **People** album to group pictures of friends and family, the **Places** album to see where your photos were taken, and then edit the best ones using the built-in tools to adjust lighting or crop out unwanted objects.

4. Notes: Stay Organized and Capture Ideas

What it is: Notes is a versatile app that helps you capture quick ideas, make to-do lists, and even store scanned documents or handwritten notes. It syncs seamlessly across all Apple devices using iCloud.

What's new: In macOS, Notes has received significant improvements, such as **locked notes** for sensitive information, **collaboration** features for sharing and editing notes with others, and the ability to add **checklists** for task management.

How it works: Notes lets you create text-based notes, to-do lists, sketches, and even add attachments like photos and PDFs. You can organize notes into folders and add tags to make finding them later easier. Plus, you can share notes with others for collaboration, making it a great tool for group projects.

How it helps:

- **Organizing your life**: Create notes for everything—from shopping lists and work reminders to brainstorming sessions.

- **Secure storage**: Lock sensitive notes with a password or Face ID for extra security.

- **Collaboration**: Share a note with a friend or coworker, and work together in real time, which is perfect for team-based projects or family plans.

Practical Example: Suppose you're planning a birthday party, and you need a checklist. You can use the **checklist feature** to keep track of tasks like booking the venue, ordering the cake, or sending invitations. With iCloud, you can access and update the checklist on your MacBook, iPhone, or iPad.

5. Calendar: Stay on Track with Your Schedule

What it is: Calendar is your go-to app for organizing your personal and professional schedules. It syncs with iCloud, allowing you to view and manage your events across all your devices.

What's new: The new **Time Zones** feature makes managing events across different time zones a breeze. You also get **birthday reminders** for contacts in your iCloud, so you never forget an important occasion again.

How it works: You can add events, set reminders, and schedule meetings, all within a clean and user-friendly interface. Calendar integrates with your email and contacts to automatically suggest times for meetings and appointments.

How it helps:

- **Productivity**: Set reminders and deadlines to keep track of meetings, events, or personal tasks.

- **Collaboration**: You can share calendars with family, friends, or coworkers, so everyone stays on the same page.

- **Customization**: Color-code your events to easily distinguish between work, personal, and other categories.

Practical Example: Let's say you have a busy week ahead with work meetings, social events, and appointments. Use **different colors** for each category—work, personal, social—and easily see your day's agenda at a glance. Set **reminders** for each event so you're always prepared.

Using Siri on Your MacBook Air M4

Siri is one of the most convenient and efficient tools built into macOS, and on your MacBook Air M4, it becomes an even more valuable assistant with its improved performance and seamless integration with your device. Whether you're juggling multiple tasks or just prefer hands-free control, Siri allows you to get things done with just your voice, freeing up your hands for other activities. In this section, we'll walk you through everything you need to know about using Siri on your MacBook Air M4, including how to activate

Siri, the commands you can use, and how Siri can help you be more productive throughout your day.

Activating Siri on Your MacBook Air M4

Getting started with Siri is easy, and there are several ways to activate it on your MacBook Air M4:

Method 1: Using the Siri Button

1. **Locate the Siri Icon**: The simplest way to activate Siri is by clicking the Siri icon in the top right corner of your screen. You'll find it in the menu bar, next to your Wi-Fi and battery icons.

2. **Click on the Icon**: Simply click the Siri icon, and Siri will pop up ready for your command.

3. **Give a Command**: Once Siri appears, you can immediately start speaking your command, and it will respond accordingly.

Method 2: Using Keyboard Shortcuts

If you prefer using the keyboard, there's a shortcut for that:

1. **Press Command + Space**: This shortcut activates Spotlight Search by default, but it can also be used to trigger Siri.

2. **Speak Your Command**: As soon as Siri activates, you can start speaking your voice command without needing to click anything. Just say your command clearly.

Method 3: "Hey Siri" Activation (Optional)

On the MacBook Air M4, you can also activate Siri with just your voice—no need to click anything or use keyboard shortcuts. However, this feature must be enabled first:

1. **Go to System Preferences**: Click on the Apple logo in the top-left corner of your screen, and select "System Preferences."

2. **Click on Siri**: In the System Preferences window, find and click on "Siri."

3. **Enable "Listen for 'Hey Siri'"**: Check the box next to "Listen for 'Hey Siri'" to allow voice activation. Once enabled, all you need to do is say "Hey Siri," and it will respond.

Using Siri to Perform Tasks

Now that you know how to activate Siri, let's dive into some of the practical and useful voice commands that will help you make the most of this hands-free assistant. From setting reminders to sending messages, Siri is a tool that can make your daily tasks simpler and more efficient.

Setting Reminders

Whether you have a meeting, need to pick up groceries, or just want to remember something important, Siri can help you create reminders quickly. Here's how you can use Siri to set reminders:

- **Example Command 1**: "Hey Siri, remind me to call mom at 3 PM."

- **Example Command 2**: "Hey Siri, remind me to pick up dry cleaning tomorrow morning."

Siri will confirm the reminder with a brief message like, "Okay, I'll remind you to call mom at 3 PM," and you're all set.

You can also ask Siri to show you your reminders, for example, "Hey Siri, what's on my to-do list for today?"

Sending Messages

No more fumbling with the keyboard—Siri can send text messages for you. Whether you need to reply to a friend, send an urgent work message, or just check in with a loved one, Siri can handle it all.

- **Example Command 1**: "Hey Siri, send a message to John saying I'm running late."

- **Example Command 2**: "Hey Siri, text Sarah 'I'll be there in 10 minutes.'"

Siri will ask for confirmation, "Would you like to send this message?" and all you have to do is reply with "Yes" or "Send," and your message is off to the recipient.

Searching the Web

Siri is fantastic for quick web searches. Whether you need to look something up during work or find the latest news, Siri can help you do it in seconds.

- **Example Command 1**: "Hey Siri, search the web for the best coffee shops near me."

- **Example Command 2**: "Hey Siri, what's the weather like today?"

- **Example Command 3**: "Hey Siri, find me some vegan dinner recipes."

Siri will open the results in your default browser, making it easy to browse without lifting a finger.

Setting Alarms and Timers

Whether you need to wake up early, set a reminder to take a break, or time a cooking session, Siri can handle all your alarm and timer needs.

- **Example Command 1**: "Hey Siri, set an alarm for 7 AM."

- **Example Command 2**: "Hey Siri, set a timer for 30 minutes."

Once you set the timer or alarm, Siri will notify you when time is up, and you'll never forget a task or miss an appointment again.

Playing Music and Controlling Media

Want to listen to your favorite song or a specific playlist? Siri can quickly play music, podcasts, or videos for you. Plus, you can control playback hands-free.

- **Example Command 1**: "Hey Siri, play some relaxing music."

- **Example Command 2**: "Hey Siri, play the latest episode of my podcast."

- **Example Command 3**: "Hey Siri, pause the music."

You can also skip tracks, adjust volume, and switch to a specific artist or album with ease. Simply say, "Hey Siri, skip to the next song," or "Hey Siri, turn up the volume."

Getting Directions and Traffic Updates

Siri can also help you get where you're going, whether you're driving or walking. Need to find the best route to a destination? Ask Siri.

- **Example Command 1**: "Hey Siri, how do I get to the nearest coffee shop?"

- **Example Command 2**: "Hey Siri, what's the traffic like on my way to work?"

Siri will bring up the directions in Apple Maps, complete with traffic updates and estimated arrival times.

Setting Calendar Events

Planning your day just got easier. Siri can add events to your calendar, so you don't have to manually type them in.

- **Example Command 1**: "Hey Siri, add a meeting with Jane tomorrow at 10 AM."

- **Example Command 2**: "Hey Siri, schedule a dentist appointment for Friday at 2 PM."

Siri will create the event, and you can even ask it to send you reminders for the event closer to the time.

Siri Tips for a Better Experience

While Siri is an incredibly powerful tool, here are some tips to make sure you're using it to its full potential:

- **Speak Clearly**: Siri works best when it can hear your voice clearly. Make sure you're speaking directly to the microphone (either built into the MacBook or an external one) and avoid speaking too quickly.

- **Use Contextual Commands**: Siri is great at understanding the context of your requests. For instance, if you're scheduling something, you can say, "Add it to my calendar" right after you mention the event, and Siri will know exactly what you mean.

- **Check Your Settings**: If Siri isn't responding as you expect, double-check your microphone settings or ensure "Hey Siri" is enabled. You can find these options under **System Preferences > Siri**.

- **Personalized Responses**: Siri can also learn from your interactions. The more you use it, the better it will understand your preferences and language.

CHAPTER 4: CUSTOMIZING YOUR MACBOOK AIR M4

Personalizing the System Preferences

When you first set up your MacBook Air M4, it's almost like you're meeting a new friend. It's sleek, it's fast, and it's ready to help you get through your daily tasks. But much like any new relationship, you might want to tweak things a bit so it feels more like *your* MacBook. Personalizing your MacBook's system preferences is the first step in truly making it yours, and it's a lot easier than you might think. Whether you want to adjust the brightness of your screen to suit your mood or switch to a more comfortable color scheme, your MacBook Air M4 gives you plenty of options to make everything just right.

Let's dive into the basic system preferences and show you how to adjust them for a more personalized experience. These settings don't just make your MacBook look better – they help improve its functionality to fit your needs.

1. Adjusting Screen Brightness

The brightness of your screen can dramatically affect how you feel and how well you see your content. Too bright, and your eyes may get tired quicker;

too dim, and you might miss details. Fortunately, the MacBook Air M4 makes it simple to adjust the screen brightness to your exact preference.

- **To adjust the screen brightness**:

  o **Using the Keyboard**: Look at the top row of keys on your keyboard. You'll notice two small sun icons, one with an upward arrow (to increase brightness) and one with a downward arrow (to decrease it). Press these keys to adjust your screen's brightness level on the fly.

  o **Using System Preferences**: If you prefer a more granular approach, you can fine-tune the brightness through the System Preferences:

    ▪ Open **System Preferences** from the Apple menu (the Apple logo in the top left corner of your screen).

    ▪ Click on **Displays**.

    ▪ Under the **Display** tab, you'll see a slider for **Brightness**. Move it left or right to adjust your screen's brightness. You can also enable the "Automatically adjust brightness" feature if you want your MacBook to adjust the screen brightness based on ambient lighting conditions.

Why does this matter? Well, adjusting the brightness based on your environment can help save battery life and improve visibility, especially in darker or brighter rooms. It's a small adjustment, but one that can make a big difference in your overall experience.

2. Changing the Wallpaper

Now that you have the basics down, let's talk about making your MacBook look more *you*. One of the easiest and most fun ways to personalize your MacBook is by changing the wallpaper. It's the first thing you see when you open your MacBook, and it can set the tone for your entire workspace.

- **To change your wallpaper**:
    - Right-click anywhere on your desktop and select **Change Desktop Background**, or go to **System Preferences** and click on **Desktop & Screen Saver**.
    - You'll see a collection of default wallpapers that Apple provides, ranging from scenic landscapes to abstract designs. But, if none of these catch your eye, you can choose an image of your own.
    - To use your own photo, click on the + button in the bottom left corner of the window to select a new folder. Browse through your photos, pick one, and click **Set Desktop Picture**.

Whether you prefer a calm nature scene, a favorite family photo, or a sleek minimalistic design, changing your wallpaper is a quick way to make your MacBook feel like yours. Plus, it's a nice mood booster every time you open your laptop.

3. Enabling Dark Mode

If you've ever used your MacBook Air at night or in a dimly lit room, you've probably noticed how bright the screen can feel, even at lower brightness levels. That's where **Dark Mode** comes in. It's a system-wide color scheme that swaps out light backgrounds for dark ones, making it easier on the eyes during late-night sessions. But Dark Mode isn't just about comfort – it can also help save battery life by using darker pixels in the display.

- **To enable Dark Mode**:

  - Open **System Preferences** from the Apple menu.

  - Click on **General**.

  - Under **Appearance**, you'll see three options: **Light**, **Dark**, and **Auto**.

    - **Light Mode** is the default setting, with white backgrounds and dark text.

    - **Dark Mode** replaces light backgrounds with dark ones and lightens the text to provide a higher contrast.

    - **Auto** automatically switches between Light and Dark Mode based on the time of day. It's a great option if you want your MacBook to adjust automatically, providing a bright interface during the day and switching to Dark Mode when it's evening.

Once you enable Dark Mode, you'll notice that not only does the desktop and system interface change, but so do compatible apps like Safari, Mail, and Messages. It's a more comfortable and aesthetically pleasing experience, especially for those late-night work sessions or binge-watching sessions on Netflix.

4. Organizing the Dock

The Dock on your MacBook Air M4 is one of the most visible elements of macOS, and it's also where you'll find your most-used apps. But the default Dock setup might not suit your needs, and that's okay – it's time to make it yours. You can resize the Dock, move it to different locations on the screen, or change the way your apps are displayed.

- **To customize your Dock**:

    o Open **System Preferences** and click on **Dock & Menu Bar**.

    o Here you can:

        - **Resize the Dock**: Use the slider to make the Dock bigger or smaller. A smaller Dock might suit you if you like to keep your desktop clean, while a larger one can give you more space for your most-used apps.

        - **Position the Dock**: You can place the Dock at the bottom, left, or right side of the screen. Changing its position can help you keep your desktop organized and make better use of screen real estate.

- **Auto-hide the Dock**: If you want to keep your screen looking tidy, enable the "**Automatically hide and show the Dock**" option. This will make the Dock disappear when not in use, only appearing when you move your mouse to the edge of the screen.

- **Minimize Windows into the App Icon**: When you minimize a window, it can either go to the right side of the Dock or shrink into its app icon. To keep things neat, you might want to enable this feature so that minimized windows stay out of sight and you can focus on what matters.

The beauty of the Dock is that it can be as minimal or as filled with apps as you want. If you're someone who likes a clean desktop, removing unused apps from the Dock can help streamline your workspace. Alternatively, if you prefer quick access to all your favorite apps, you can organize them by category or importance.

Why These Settings Matter

Personalizing your MacBook Air M4's system preferences doesn't just make your device look better – it helps improve how you interact with it on a daily basis. Whether you're adjusting the brightness to avoid eye strain or enabling Dark Mode for a more comfortable evening experience, these small tweaks go a long way in enhancing your overall productivity and comfort.

Changing your wallpaper makes your MacBook feel more like an extension of your personality, while organizing the Dock ensures you're only a click away from the apps you use most. These settings are simple, but they add up to a vastly improved user experience, one that reflects your style and needs.

So, take a moment to explore the System Preferences, and don't be afraid to experiment. After all, your MacBook Air M4 is designed to be as flexible and customizable as you are.

Setting Up Touch ID and FaceTime

The MacBook Air M4 brings with it an array of powerful features, but two that stand out for enhancing both security and communication are **Touch ID** and **FaceTime**. Whether you're looking to speed up logins with your fingerprint or make crystal-clear video calls to friends and colleagues, both features are designed to streamline your experience. Let's dive into setting them up and making the most of these essential tools!

Setting Up Touch ID on Your MacBook Air M4

Touch ID is a feature that lets you use your fingerprint to unlock your MacBook, make payments, and access certain apps. It's not only convenient but also a secure way to keep your MacBook safe from unauthorized access. Here's how to set it up:

1. Open System Preferences

- Start by clicking the **Apple logo** in the top-left corner of your screen.

- From the drop-down menu, select **System Preferences**.

2. Navigate to Touch ID Settings

- In the System Preferences window, look for the **Touch ID** icon and click on it. This will take you to the Touch ID settings where you can manage your fingerprints and how Touch ID interacts with your MacBook.

3. Add a Fingerprint

- You'll be prompted to **add a fingerprint**. Click the **Add Fingerprint** button to get started.

- Now, position your finger on the **Touch ID sensor** (located on the top-right corner of your MacBook Air's keyboard).

- Gently press your finger on the sensor and lift it off when prompted. You'll need to repeat this process several times, adjusting your finger slightly each time to ensure the sensor captures different angles of your fingerprint.

4. Complete the Setup

- Once your fingerprint is registered, you'll be asked to choose what actions you'd like to use Touch ID for. You can enable Touch ID to:

- o **Unlock your Mac**: Allow your MacBook to unlock with just a touch of your finger.

- o **Make payments**: Use Touch ID for Apple Pay transactions.

- o **Use it with apps and passwords**: Some apps or websites will allow you to authenticate actions using Touch ID for convenience.

Check the boxes according to your preference. You can always change this later by revisiting the Touch ID settings.

5. Test Touch ID

- After the setup, try unlocking your MacBook by simply placing your finger on the Touch ID sensor. The MacBook should unlock almost instantly, making the login process much faster.

- If you added more than one fingerprint, feel free to test each finger to make sure they all work.

Tips for Using Touch ID:

- **Cleaning the Sensor**: Touch ID sensors can accumulate dust or oil from your fingers, so it's a good idea to gently clean the sensor with a microfiber cloth every so often.

- **Adding Multiple Fingers**: You can add up to **three fingerprints** for different fingers or hands. If you find that Touch ID isn't as responsive with one finger, try registering a new one.

- **Security**: Touch ID is incredibly secure, using sophisticated encryption to keep your data private. Rest assured, your fingerprint data is stored securely on your Mac and not in the cloud.

Setting Up FaceTime on Your MacBook Air M4

FaceTime is Apple's built-in video and audio calling app that allows you to connect with friends, family, and colleagues with ease. Whether you're having a quick chat or a full-on video conference, FaceTime makes staying in touch simple and reliable. Let's get started with setting it up:

1. Open the FaceTime App

- To begin, click on the **Launchpad** icon in your Dock, or use **Spotlight** by pressing **Command + Space** and typing in "FaceTime."

- Open the **FaceTime app**.

2. Sign In with Your Apple ID

- If you haven't already signed in, FaceTime will prompt you to do so. Enter the **Apple ID** you use for other Apple services like iCloud, iTunes, or the App Store.

- If you don't have an Apple ID yet, you can create one directly through the app by following the on-screen instructions.

3. Enable FaceTime on Your MacBook

- After signing in, you can choose which methods you want to use for receiving FaceTime calls. You'll typically be asked if you want to be reachable via your **phone number** and **email address**.

- Check the boxes next to the options that apply to you. For example, if you want to be reachable on your email address (i.e., if you don't want to link your phone number to FaceTime on your Mac), simply select **your email**.

4. Setting Up Audio and Video Calling Preferences

- Now, let's set up FaceTime for both **audio** and **video** calls. To ensure everything works smoothly:

  - **Video Calling**: Ensure that the **camera** is functioning properly by testing it during a video call. You can access your camera settings via the **Camera** section in **System Preferences**.

  - **Audio Calling**: If you plan to use FaceTime for audio calls, make sure your **microphone** is active. You can check this by going into the **Sound** settings in **System Preferences** and ensuring the input device is set correctly.

5. Make Your First Call

- Once everything is set up, it's time to make your first call!

  - **To make a video call**, open the FaceTime app and type in the phone number or email address of the person you want to call.

- When their contact appears, click the **video camera icon** to start a video call.

- For an audio call, click the **phone icon** instead.

6. Managing FaceTime Calls

- During a call, you'll see several options:

  - **Mute Microphone**: Tap the microphone icon to mute your voice.

  - **Camera On/Off**: Tap the camera icon to turn your video on or off during the call.

  - **End Call**: Tap the red phone icon to hang up the call when you're done.

7. Use FaceTime with Other Apple Devices

- If you have an iPhone, iPad, or even an Apple Watch, you can use FaceTime to seamlessly transition between devices.

  - For instance, you can start a FaceTime call on your iPhone and pick it up later on your MacBook, or even continue a call on your Apple Watch if you're away from your MacBook.

Tips for Using FaceTime:

- **Camera Positioning**: If you're making a video call, ensure the camera is angled well, ideally at eye level, for the best video quality.

- **FaceTime Audio Quality**: When on audio calls, make sure you're in a quiet space for the best call clarity.

- **FaceTime with Groups**: FaceTime also supports group calls, allowing you to chat with multiple people at once. To start a group call, simply add more contacts to the call as you would a one-on-one FaceTime call.

Conclusion: Why Touch ID and FaceTime Make Your MacBook Air M4 Even Better

Setting up **Touch ID** and **FaceTime** on your MacBook Air M4 not only adds layers of security and convenience, but they also open up new ways to communicate and protect your device. Touch ID streamlines your logins and transactions, making your MacBook feel more secure and personal, while FaceTime ensures that staying in touch with loved ones or colleagues is just a few clicks away.

With **Touch ID**, you're adding a quick and secure way to access your MacBook, and with **FaceTime**, you're equipped for both one-on-one conversations and group calls, all with high-quality video and audio. These features are not only intuitive to use but are also key to creating a more seamless and connected experience, whether you're working from home or catching up with family.

Now that you've got Touch ID and FaceTime set up, you're all ready to get the most out of your MacBook Air M4. Let these powerful features simplify your life and make your MacBook experience even more enjoyable.

Integrating with the Apple Ecosystem: iCloud, iPhone, and iPad

One of the most exciting features of owning a MacBook Air M4 is its seamless integration with the rest of the Apple ecosystem. Apple has created a sophisticated system that allows all its devices to work together as if they were one. Whether you're moving from your iPhone to your MacBook Air or accessing a file from your iPad while working on your MacBook, this integration makes life easier and more efficient. In this section, we'll dive into how you can take full advantage of iCloud and connect your MacBook Air M4 with your iPhone and iPad for a smooth and connected experience.

What is iCloud and Why Should You Use It?

iCloud is Apple's cloud service that securely stores your data, such as photos, documents, contacts, calendars, and more, and automatically syncs it across all your Apple devices. Think of iCloud as a virtual bridge that ties together your iPhone, iPad, MacBook, and even your Apple Watch, so your files, contacts, and settings are always up to date.

When you set up iCloud on your MacBook Air M4, you create a seamless experience between your devices, which means you can start a task on one device and pick it up on another. This connection is more than just convenience—it's about creating a consistent, fluid workflow that makes using your devices together feel effortless.

Setting Up iCloud on Your MacBook Air M4

Setting up iCloud on your MacBook Air M4 is straightforward and only takes a few minutes. Here's how to get started:

1. **Open System Preferences**: Click the Apple logo in the top-left corner of your screen and choose "System Preferences."

2. **Sign in with Your Apple ID**: In the System Preferences window, click on "Apple ID" and sign in with your Apple ID credentials. If you don't have an Apple ID, you'll be prompted to create one.

3. **Enable iCloud**: Once you're signed in, click the "iCloud" tab in the sidebar. You'll see a list of features and services that you can sync across your Apple devices. These include iCloud Drive, Contacts, Calendars, Notes, Safari, and more. Simply check the boxes next to the services you want to sync.

4. **Manage Your iCloud Storage**: iCloud offers 5GB of free storage, but if you need more space to store photos, videos, and documents, you can purchase additional storage through the iCloud settings.

With iCloud set up, your MacBook Air M4 will automatically sync your data across all devices. Here's what happens next:

- **Photos**: Any photos you take on your iPhone or iPad will automatically appear on your MacBook Air in the Photos app. No more emailing photos to yourself or manually transferring files. iCloud Photos ensures everything is instantly available on every device.

- **Contacts and Calendars**: Your contacts, calendar events, and reminders are shared across devices, so you'll always have your most up-to-date information no matter which device you're using.

- **Files**: iCloud Drive allows you to store documents in the cloud, so you can access them from any device. If you're working on a file on your MacBook Air, you can continue where you left off on your iPhone or iPad without any interruptions. Whether you're writing a report, reviewing a presentation, or editing photos, iCloud Drive ensures all your files are synchronized.

Using Handoff Between Your MacBook Air M4, iPhone, and iPad

Handoff is one of the standout features of the Apple ecosystem. This feature lets you start an activity on one device and then pick it up on another without missing a beat. Here's how it works:

- **Start on iPhone, Finish on MacBook**: Imagine you're typing an email on your iPhone while on the go. Once you sit down at your MacBook Air M4, you'll notice a small icon of the app (Mail, for example) appear in the bottom-left corner of your MacBook screen. You can simply click on it and continue composing the email on your MacBook.

- **Start on Mac, Finish on iPad**: Similarly, you could begin writing a document on your MacBook and then switch to your iPad when you're in a different environment. The document will seamlessly

MACBOOK AIR M4 USER GUIDE

transition from the MacBook to the iPad without any extra effort on your part.

For this to work, Handoff must be enabled on all your devices. To check if it's activated:

1. Go to **System Preferences** on your MacBook Air M4, click **General**, and ensure that "Allow Handoff between this Mac and your iCloud devices" is checked.

2. On your iPhone or iPad, navigate to **Settings** > **General** > **AirPlay & Handoff** and toggle on Handoff.

With Handoff, you can easily continue activities like reading, writing, and browsing between devices, making it a game-changer for anyone who switches between multiple Apple devices throughout the day.

AirDrop: Sharing Files Instantly Between Devices

AirDrop is Apple's fast, secure way to share files between devices without needing an internet connection or any physical cables. You can share documents, photos, links, and even contacts between your MacBook Air M4, iPhone, and iPad with just a few taps.

Here's how to use AirDrop:

1. **Enable AirDrop on Your Devices**: On your MacBook, open Finder, click "Go" in the menu bar, and select "AirDrop." On your iPhone or iPad, swipe down to open the Control Center, then tap the AirDrop

icon. Make sure both devices have AirDrop set to "Everyone" or "Contacts Only."

2. **Send Files**: To share a file, simply drag it to the AirDrop window on your MacBook or tap the share icon on your iPhone/iPad and select the device you want to send it to.

3. **Receive Files**: If someone sends you a file via AirDrop, a notification will pop up on your MacBook, iPhone, or iPad asking if you'd like to accept the file. Click "Accept," and the file will instantly appear in the appropriate app (e.g., Photos, Documents).

AirDrop is a great way to quickly send pictures from your iPhone to your MacBook or share a document from your MacBook to your iPad. The best part is, everything happens instantly and wirelessly.

Universal Clipboard: Copy and Paste Across Devices

With Universal Clipboard, Apple makes copying and pasting across devices a breeze. Copy something on your iPhone or iPad, and you can paste it on your MacBook Air M4, and vice versa.

Here's how it works:

1. **Copy**: On your iPhone or iPad, copy text, an image, or a file.

2. **Paste**: On your MacBook, press Command+V to paste it wherever you need it. Similarly, you can copy something from your MacBook and paste it on your iPhone.

This makes tasks like copying a phone number from your iPhone and pasting it into a document on your MacBook, or copying a link from Safari on your iPad and pasting it into an email on your MacBook, incredibly smooth and quick.

Using iMessage and FaceTime Across Devices

iMessage and FaceTime are core Apple services that work across your Apple devices. Whether you're at your desk with your MacBook Air M4 or on the go with your iPhone, you can send messages and make video calls seamlessly.

- **iMessage**: If you're having a conversation on your iPhone, you can switch to your MacBook and continue the conversation without missing a beat. Just open the Messages app on your MacBook, and all your texts will sync instantly.

- **FaceTime**: Likewise, FaceTime calls are fully integrated across your devices. You can start a FaceTime call on your iPhone, and if you want to switch to a bigger screen, simply pick it up on your MacBook. The call will transfer seamlessly.

Benefits of the Apple Ecosystem

The beauty of the Apple ecosystem lies in its simplicity and continuity. Here's how it benefits you:

- **Efficiency**: With features like Handoff and Universal Clipboard, you can switch between devices without missing a step. You can start a task on your iPhone and finish it on your MacBook, saving you time and hassle.

- **Synchronization**: iCloud ensures your files, photos, contacts, and apps are always in sync across all your devices, so you never have to worry about manually transferring content.

- **Convenience**: AirDrop, Handoff, and Universal Clipboard make it easy to share files and copy/paste content between your devices. These features work seamlessly in the background, allowing you to focus on what matters most.

- **Communication**: With iMessage and FaceTime integrated across all your Apple devices, staying connected with friends and family becomes effortless. You can answer messages or calls from any device, whether you're at home or on the go.

CHAPTER 5: ADVANCED MACOS FEATURES

Working with Multiple Desktops and Split View

One of the most powerful features in macOS is the ability to manage multiple desktops and use Split View. If you're someone who juggles multiple tasks at once, this feature can be a game-changer. Whether you're working on a project that requires having several documents open or simply want to keep your communication app separate from your work files, multiple desktops and Split View can help you stay organized and maximize your productivity. Let's dive into how you can use these features to streamline your workflow.

What Are Multiple Desktops?

Multiple desktops, also known as *Spaces*, allow you to create several virtual desktops on your MacBook Air M4, each with its own set of open apps and windows. This feature gives you the freedom to separate your work tasks into different "spaces," making it easy to switch between them and stay focused. For instance, you might want to have one desktop for emails and meetings, another for creative work or document writing, and a third for research. By organizing tasks this way, you avoid clutter and improve your efficiency.

Setting Up Multiple Desktops

Getting started with multiple desktops is easy. Here's how you can set them up:

1. **Open Mission Control**:

   o You can access Mission Control by swiping up with three or four fingers on your trackpad or by pressing the F3 key on your MacBook Air's keyboard. Mission Control gives you an overview of all open windows and allows you to manage your desktops.

2. **Add a New Desktop**:

   o At the top of your screen, you'll see a row of desktops, each represented by a thumbnail. To add a new desktop, move your cursor to the top-right corner of the screen and click the + button. This will create a new desktop space for you.

3. **Switch Between Desktops**:

   o Once you have multiple desktops set up, you can easily switch between them by swiping left or right with three fingers on your trackpad. You can also access your desktops in Mission Control by clicking on the desired desktop thumbnail.

4. **Move Apps Between Desktops**:

   o To move an open app or window to another desktop, enter Mission Control, then drag the app's window to the desktop thumbnail you want it on. You can quickly organize your workspace by placing related apps together on different desktops.

Why Use Multiple Desktops?

Multiple desktops help keep your workflow organized and prevent your screen from feeling cluttered. Here are some reasons why using multiple desktops can be a huge benefit:

- **Task Segmentation**: If you're working on multiple projects, you can create separate desktops for each task. For example, you could have one desktop dedicated to reading research articles, another for writing a report, and another for checking emails or messages.

- **Quick Task Switching**: With multiple desktops, you can switch between tasks quickly without having to minimize or search for windows. This speeds up your workflow, as you don't have to waste time looking for open applications.

- **Focus and Productivity**: Keeping apps separated and organized into different desktops helps you focus on one thing at a time. You're not distracted by unrelated tasks or windows, and everything you need for a specific task is contained within a single desktop.

Working with Split View

While multiple desktops are excellent for managing tasks across different spaces, Split View is perfect for multitasking within a single desktop. Split View allows you to fill the screen with two apps side by side, each taking up half of the screen. This is especially useful when you need to compare information from two sources or work in two apps simultaneously.

Here's how to use Split View on your MacBook Air M4:

1. **Enter Split View**:

   o First, open the two apps you want to use in Split View. Hover your mouse over the green maximize button (the one in the top-left corner) of one of the apps. You'll see two options: **Tile Window to Left of Screen** or **Tile Window to Right of Screen**. Choose one of these options to snap the app to the left or right side of your screen.

2. **Choose the Second App**:

   o After the first app has snapped into place, you'll be prompted to select a second app. Click on the app you want to use on the other side of the screen, and it will automatically fill the remaining space.

3. **Adjust the Divider**:

   o Once you're in Split View, you can adjust the divider between the two apps by dragging it left or right. This allows you to customize how much screen space each app gets, based on your preferences.

4. **Exit Split View**:

   o To exit Split View, simply click the green button on either app again, or swipe up with three fingers to open Mission Control. From there, you can click on any of the apps to exit Split View and return to your regular desktop view.

Why Use Split View?

Split View is a fantastic tool for multitasking because it allows you to focus on two tasks simultaneously without constantly switching between windows. Here are a few examples of how Split View can enhance productivity:

- **Comparing Documents**: If you're writing a report and need to reference a source document, you can have both documents open side by side. No more flipping between tabs or windows—you can see both at once, making it easier to compare and gather information.

- **Managing Communication**: For people who need to keep up with messages, emails, or chats while working, Split View allows you to have your email app or messaging platform open on one side and your work app on the other, so you can respond without interrupting your workflow.

- **Editing and Viewing**: If you're editing a photo or video and need to review a reference, Split View lets you keep your editing software open alongside a browser window, video player, or reference document.

Tips for Organizing Windows and Maximizing Productivity

To make the most out of multiple desktops and Split View, here are some helpful tips:

1. **Group Related Apps Together**:

   o   For maximum efficiency, group apps by task. For example, you can have a desktop dedicated to research (with Safari and Notes open), one for writing (with Microsoft Word or Pages), and another for communication (with Slack or Mail). This prevents distraction and keeps your workflow streamlined.

2. **Use Mission Control to Monitor Your Workspace**:

   o   Mission Control is a great way to get a bird's-eye view of all your open desktops and windows. If you're juggling multiple tasks, use Mission Control to quickly locate and switch between apps or spaces.

3. **Keep Key Apps in Split View**:

   o   If there are certain apps you use frequently together (like a calendar and a task manager, or a web browser and a word processor), keep them in Split View for easy access. This will save you the time and effort of switching between multiple apps.

4. **Utilize Hot Corners and Gestures**:

   o You can set up Hot Corners in your system preferences, which allow you to quickly trigger certain actions like Mission Control or launching the screen saver by simply moving your mouse to a corner of the screen. Pair this with trackpad gestures for even faster multitasking.

5. **Remember to Stay Organized**:

   o With so many windows and desktops, it's easy to feel overwhelmed. Be mindful of your workspace and avoid opening unnecessary apps or tabs. Use shortcuts like Command + Tab to quickly switch between open apps, and try to keep your desktops organized to prevent clutter.

Boosting Productivity with Keyboard Shortcuts and Gestures

In this section, we're diving into two of the most powerful yet often underutilized features of your MacBook Air M4: **keyboard shortcuts** and **touchpad gestures**. These little gems can drastically improve the way you work, allowing you to perform tasks faster and more efficiently. Once you master these, you'll wonder how you ever got by without them. So, let's break them down in a way that's easy to understand, with real-life examples and practical tips for integrating them into your workflow.

Keyboard Shortcuts: The Ultimate Time-Savers

Keyboard shortcuts are your secret weapon when it comes to boosting productivity. Think of them as your fast lane to get things done without having to fumble through menus or click endlessly. Instead of spending time navigating with a mouse or trackpad, you can perform actions with just a couple of keystrokes.

Here are some **essential keyboard shortcuts** to help you breeze through your daily tasks on the MacBook Air M4:

1. Basic Navigation Shortcuts

- **Command (⌘) + Tab**: Switch between open apps. This one's perfect when you've got multiple programs running and need to quickly hop between them without reaching for the mouse.

- **Command (⌘) + Q**: Close an app. If you're done with an app and don't need it cluttering your screen, hit ⌘ + **Q** to close it instantly. You'll be amazed at how much more organized your workspace feels.

- **Command (⌘) + Space**: Open Spotlight Search. Whether you're searching for an app, file, or even a web page, **Spotlight** is your go-to search tool. Just type a few letters, and Spotlight will find it for you—fast.

- **Command (⌘) + H**: Hide the active window. If you need to quickly hide a window without closing it, hit **⌘ + H**. This is especially helpful when you need to focus on a specific app without distractions.

2. File Management Shortcuts

- **Command (⌘) + C**: Copy. This is one of the most fundamental shortcuts, allowing you to copy text or files with ease.

- **Command (⌘) + V**: Paste. Once you've copied something, **⌘ + V** will let you paste it wherever you need.

- **Command (⌘) + X**: Cut. When you need to move something instead of just copying it, **⌘ + X** will cut it from its current location and allow you to paste it somewhere else.

- **Command (⌘) + Shift + N**: Create a new folder in Finder. A quick way to organize your files on the fly.

- **Command (⌘) + Delete**: Move items to the trash. If you're tidying up your desktop or file folders, this shortcut will quickly send any selected file to the trash bin.

3. Window Management Shortcuts

- **Command (⌘) + M**: Minimize the active window. If you want to keep an app open but out of sight, simply hit **⌘ + M** to minimize it to the dock.

- **Command (⌘) + W**: Close the current window. Unlike ⌘ + **Q**, which closes an entire app, ⌘ + **W** will only close the current window you're working on.

- **Command (⌘) + Option + M**: Minimize all windows of the active app. If you have a ton of windows open for a single app and need a quick cleanup, this shortcut will send them all to the dock at once.

4. Text Editing Shortcuts

- **Command (⌘) + A**: Select all. This is a lifesaver when you want to select everything in a document or on a webpage without manually dragging your cursor across everything.

- **Command (⌘) + Z**: Undo. Made a mistake? ⌘ + **Z** is here to rescue you, undoing your last action—whether you accidentally deleted something or just need to go back a step.

- **Command (⌘) + Shift + Z**: Redo. If you changed your mind and want to reverse the undo, use ⌘ + **Shift + Z** to redo it.

- **Command (⌘) + F**: Find. Whether you're searching within a document or looking for a word on a webpage, ⌘ + **F** opens the find bar, allowing you to search for specific text.

Touchpad Gestures: Navigate Like a Pro

Now, let's talk about your MacBook Air M4's **trackpad**—it's not just for moving the cursor around. The trackpad on the M4 is incredibly responsive, and with a few simple gestures, you can perform tasks that might otherwise take several clicks. Let's explore some **powerful touchpad gestures** that will make you feel like a MacBook pro in no time.

1. Basic Gestures

- **Click**: Tap the trackpad with one finger to select items or open apps. It's as simple as it sounds, but mastering this is the foundation for using other gestures effectively.

- **Right-click**: Tap the trackpad with two fingers to bring up context menus. If you're used to right-clicking with a mouse, this gesture will feel familiar but with the added convenience of not needing an actual mouse.

- **Scroll**: Swipe two fingers up or down to scroll through documents, webpages, or lists. The trackpad makes it smooth and intuitive, mimicking the scrolling motion you'd use on your phone.

- **Zoom**: Pinch with two fingers to zoom in or out on photos, web pages, or maps. This is perfect for quickly adjusting the view without having to mess with buttons or settings.

2. Advanced Gestures

- **Mission Control**: Swipe up with three fingers to open Mission Control, which shows all your open windows, apps, and desktops. This is perfect for multitasking and organizing your workspace with ease.

- **Switching Between Apps**: Swipe left or right with three fingers to quickly switch between open applications. This is a game-changer for anyone who juggles multiple apps at once, like writing a document while researching online.

- **Show Desktop**: Spread three fingers apart to reveal the desktop, minimizing all windows. This is incredibly useful when you need to access files or folders quickly without closing everything.

- **App Exposé**: Swipe down with three fingers to see all open windows within the current app. This is particularly helpful when you have multiple windows from the same app and need to quickly switch between them.

3. Custom Gestures

- **Set Custom Shortcuts**: You can customize your trackpad gestures to suit your workflow better. For instance, you might want to assign specific gestures for opening certain apps or documents. Go to **System Preferences > Trackpad > More Gestures** and set it up to fit your needs.

- **Force Touch**: The MacBook Air M4's trackpad also features Force Touch, which allows you to click harder for additional options, like previewing links or using quick actions. This gives you even more control over your experience.

Integrating Shortcuts and Gestures into Your Workflow

Now that we've covered the essential keyboard shortcuts and touchpad gestures, it's time to integrate them into your workflow. The key here is consistency—once you start using these shortcuts and gestures regularly, they'll become second nature, allowing you to navigate macOS with ease.

Here's a simple plan for integrating these features into your daily routine:

1. **Start with the basics**: Begin by incorporating just a few of the most useful shortcuts (like **Command + C** for copy, **Command + V** for paste, and **Command + Tab** for switching apps) into your daily tasks. These are the most commonly used shortcuts and will already make a significant difference.

2. **Gradually add more**: As you get more comfortable, start using additional shortcuts, like those for file management or window navigation. Experiment with the touchpad gestures to see which ones resonate with you the most.

3. **Customize your gestures**: If there's a gesture or shortcut that could improve your efficiency further, take the time to customize it to fit your needs. Whether it's setting up custom shortcuts for apps or assigning new gestures for quicker access to documents, macOS lets you tailor your experience.

4. **Stay consistent**: The more you use these features, the more you'll see how much time they save. Stick with it, and soon, you won't even have to think about using them—they'll become second nature.

Using Siri Shortcuts to Automate Tasks

In today's fast-paced world, efficiency is key. One of the most powerful tools on your MacBook Air M4 to boost productivity is Siri Shortcuts. Whether you're an experienced Mac user or just getting started, Siri Shortcuts is a game-changer. It allows you to automate tasks, so you don't have to manually do the same actions over and over again. Let's dive into how you can set up and use Siri Shortcuts to automate tasks and make your day-to-day workflow much smoother.

What Are Siri Shortcuts?

At its core, Siri Shortcuts are a series of actions that you can automate with just a simple voice command or by tapping on the Shortcut from your device. These actions can include things like sending a message, opening a website, adjusting settings, or even performing multiple actions with a single tap. Siri Shortcuts not only works with your MacBook but also integrates seamlessly with your iPhone, iPad, and Apple Watch, creating a cohesive Apple ecosystem where your devices work together to save you time.

Setting Up Siri Shortcuts on Your MacBook Air M4

Before you can start automating your tasks, you'll need to set up Siri Shortcuts. Luckily, macOS makes it incredibly easy to get started.

1. **Open the Shortcuts App:**

o The first thing you'll need to do is open the **Shortcuts** app on your MacBook Air M4. You can find it by clicking on the **Launchpad** or searching for it in **Spotlight**.

o If you're using macOS for the first time, you might not have any shortcuts set up yet, but don't worry; we'll go over how to create new ones.

2. **Familiarizing Yourself with the Interface:**

o When you open the Shortcuts app, you'll see a clean, user-friendly interface. On the left side, you have a library of all the shortcuts you've created or downloaded. On the right, you'll see a preview of the shortcut you select.

o You can start creating shortcuts either by choosing from the **Gallery** (pre-made shortcuts) or by creating your own **Personal Shortcut**.

3. **Creating Your First Shortcut:**

o To create a shortcut from scratch, click the + button at the top-right of the app. This opens a blank shortcut editor.

o You'll see a list of **Actions** on the left. These actions can range from opening apps to controlling settings on your Mac.

o Drag and drop the actions you want to use into the shortcut editor on the right. For example, if you want to create a shortcut that opens your favorite website and sends a reminder at the same time, you would:

- Select the **Open URL** action and type in the website link.

- Then add the **Show Reminder** action to remind you to check that website later.

o Once your actions are set up, click **Done** at the top-right to save the shortcut.

4. **Running Your Shortcut:**

o Now that you've created a shortcut, you can run it by either:

- Clicking on the **Shortcut** directly from the Shortcuts app.

- Using **Siri** by saying, "Hey Siri, [Shortcut Name]." This will trigger the shortcut automatically.

- Assigning the shortcut to a specific keyboard shortcut for even quicker access.

- Adding the shortcut to your MacBook's **menu bar** for easy access at any time.

Examples of Tasks You Can Automate with Siri Shortcuts

Now that you know how to set up your shortcuts, let's look at some real-life examples of how you can use Siri Shortcuts to save time and increase efficiency.

1. Automating Your Morning Routine

Imagine waking up and starting your day with everything ready for you. You can create a shortcut that runs multiple actions at once, like this:

- **Action 1:** Turn off **Do Not Disturb**.

- **Action 2:** Open your favorite news website.

- **Action 3:** Set your calendar reminders for the day.

- **Action 4:** Play your favorite morning playlist on Apple Music.

To set this up, simply create a new shortcut with each action listed above, and when you say, "Hey Siri, good morning," Siri will perform all these tasks at once.

2. Setting Up a Work-from-Home Shortcut

If you're working from home, your day likely starts with a few essential tasks. Instead of doing them manually, automate it all with a shortcut. Here's an example:

- **Action 1:** Open **Zoom** for your meetings.

- **Action 2:** Set your Mac to **Do Not Disturb** to minimize distractions.

- **Action 3:** Turn on your work playlist to help you concentrate.

Now, when you say, "Hey Siri, start my workday," your MacBook will open Zoom, silence notifications, and start your music—all with one simple command.

3. Automating Your Evening Routine

After a long day, you might want to unwind. With Siri Shortcuts, you can set an evening routine that takes care of everything for you:

- **Action 1:** Turn off **Wi-Fi** to disconnect from work.

- **Action 2:** Start a **relaxing playlist** in Apple Music.

- **Action 3:** Set a **bedtime reminder** for the next day.

- **Action 4:** Set your **Mac to sleep** after 30 minutes.

You can activate this routine by saying, "Hey Siri, start my evening," and your MacBook will do the rest, helping you disconnect and relax.

4. Quickly Sending a Text or Email

Sending a quick text or email doesn't have to be a hassle. With Siri Shortcuts, you can set up a shortcut to send messages with minimal effort:

- **Action 1:** Create a shortcut that sends a pre-written text message or email to a specific contact.

- **Action 2:** Customize the message with variable fields like today's date or an appointment.

Now, when you need to send a quick reminder or update, you can just say, "Hey Siri, send my reminder," and Siri will take care of it for you.

5. Controlling Your Smart Home Devices

If you have smart home devices like lights, thermostats, or smart plugs, you can use Siri Shortcuts to control them all with a voice command. Here's an example:

- **Action 1:** Turn off the lights.

- **Action 2:** Adjust the thermostat.

- **Action 3:** Lock the front door.

You can create a shortcut called "Goodnight" that, when triggered, will do all of these actions automatically. Just say, "Hey Siri, goodnight," and your MacBook will control all your smart devices.

Advanced Automation: Combining Multiple Apps

Siri Shortcuts really shines when you combine multiple apps and actions. For example, if you're working on a project, you can create a shortcut that:

- Opens your **project management app**.

- Sends a reminder to **Slack** to notify your team.

- Opens your **Google Drive** folder with project documents.

This kind of multi-step automation helps streamline tasks that usually require multiple actions, allowing you to accomplish a lot with minimal effort.

Troubleshooting Siri Shortcuts

While Siri Shortcuts is incredibly reliable, sometimes things might not work as expected. Here are a few troubleshooting tips:

- **Shortcut Not Working?** Make sure the actions in your shortcut are set up correctly and that your apps are up-to-date.

- **Siri Not Recognizing Your Command?** Ensure your shortcut is named something Siri can easily recognize. Try testing it with a different phrase or adjusting the shortcut's name for clarity.

- **Permission Issues:** Some actions, like sending a message or email, might require additional permissions. Be sure to grant the necessary permissions when prompted.

Final Thoughts on Siri Shortcuts

Siri Shortcuts are more than just a novelty feature—they're a powerful way to make your MacBook Air M4 work smarter for you. From automating daily routines to integrating with your smart home, the possibilities are virtually endless. Once you get the hang of setting up your own shortcuts, you'll wonder how you ever lived without them.

Start small with simple tasks, and soon you'll be automating your entire workflow. By taking advantage of Siri Shortcuts, you'll not only save time but also enjoy a more seamless and productive experience on your MacBook Air M4.

MacBook Air M4 for Professionals: Advanced Features for Power Users

The MacBook Air M4 is not just a sleek, lightweight device perfect for everyday tasks; it's also a powerhouse designed to handle the demanding needs of professionals. Whether you're a coder, a video editor, or a graphic designer, the MacBook Air M4 can support the tools you rely on for high-performance tasks. Thanks to the new M4 chip and macOS optimizations, this model is equipped to handle professional-grade software and workflows with ease. Let's dive into how the MacBook Air M4 can support your advanced professional tasks.

1. Coding and Development: Powering the Developer's Workflow

For developers, coding is a blend of creativity and precision. Whether you're working with Xcode for macOS/iOS development, Python for data science, or using frameworks like React for web development, the MacBook Air M4 is more than capable of meeting your needs.

The M4 Chip: A Game-Changer for Developers
With the M4 chip at its core, the MacBook Air M4 offers an incredible balance of power and efficiency. The chip's improved architecture accelerates compiling times, making your development tasks much quicker and smoother. It ensures that your workflow remains uninterrupted, even

when you're working on resource-intensive tasks like compiling code, running multiple virtual environments, or debugging in real-time.

macOS   Features   for   Development

macOS is a developer's dream. Integrated with powerful tools like **Xcode**, **Terminal**, and **Homebrew**, macOS provides an environment optimized for coding. The MacBook Air M4 runs all the necessary software tools smoothly, making it an ideal choice for software engineers, app developers, and web developers alike.

- **Terminal and Homebrew**: These essential tools let developers control their environments and install open-source software with ease. The MacBook Air M4's performance ensures that even when you're managing complex dependencies or working with large repositories, it won't slow down.

- **Xcode**: For iOS and macOS development, Xcode is essential, and the MacBook Air M4's M4 chip makes running this resource-heavy app a seamless experience. With the faster performance of the M4 chip, you can expect swift application builds, improved testing environments, and a more fluid coding experience.

- **Virtualization and Containerization**: The M4 chip's efficiency makes running virtual machines, Docker containers, and even emulators more practical on a MacBook Air M4. Whether you're testing applications on different operating systems or managing complex software environments, the MacBook Air M4 handles these processes smoothly, with no lag or stutter.

In essence, for coding professionals, the MacBook Air M4 is built to handle both the heavy lifting of development and the speed necessary to keep up with rapid deployment times and continuous development cycles.

2. Video Editing: A Powerhouse for Creators

For creative professionals working in video production, the MacBook Air M4's M4 chip is a revelation. Video editing software like **Final Cut Pro**, **Adobe Premiere Pro**, and **DaVinci Resolve** all demand a significant amount of power and processing speed. The MacBook Air M4, with its enhanced M4 chip, offers top-tier performance for video editing, even when working with 4K footage or complex projects that require heavy rendering.

The   M4   Chip's   Graphics   Performance
One of the standout features of the MacBook Air M4 for video editing is the **M4 chip's graphics capabilities**. With an integrated GPU designed to handle advanced graphics and render video effects smoothly, video editors can expect smooth playback, faster rendering, and less lag in between edits. The MacBook Air M4 handles demanding tasks like color grading, transitions, and visual effects without skipping a beat, ensuring that video editors can work at a professional level.

macOS   Features   for   Video   Editing
macOS is well-equipped to support professional-grade video editing. Tools like **Final Cut Pro X** and **iMovie** are optimized for macOS and run smoothly on the MacBook Air M4. But it doesn't stop there—macOS also supports a wide range of third-party video editing software like Adobe Premiere and

DaVinci Resolve. With its ability to handle these heavy-duty applications, macOS truly shines in the world of video editing.

- **Metal Framework**: The Metal framework in macOS ensures that graphics-intensive applications, such as those used in video editing, run efficiently on the MacBook Air M4. Metal reduces the overhead that slows down performance in high-end software, ensuring that video editors get real-time feedback as they edit, no matter how complex the footage may be.

- **Storage and Organization**: Video files can be large and cumbersome, but the MacBook Air M4's fast **SSD storage** makes file access and transfers incredibly fast. When editing video, the ability to quickly retrieve and save large video files can significantly improve workflow efficiency. Additionally, the integration of **iCloud Drive** ensures that your files are always backed up and accessible, even if you're working remotely or on the go.

3. Graphic Design: Precision and Performance for Designers

Graphic designers will appreciate the MacBook Air M4's ability to handle design software like **Adobe Photoshop**, **Illustrator**, and **Affinity Designer** with ease. Whether you're designing high-resolution graphics, working on detailed illustrations, or retouching photos, the MacBook Air M4 provides the power needed for professional design work.

High-Resolution   Display   and   Color   Accuracy
The MacBook Air M4's Retina display is another significant advantage for

graphic designers. With **True Tone technology** and a high-resolution screen, the display offers vibrant colors and precise details, making it perfect for photo editing, web design, or digital painting. The high pixel density ensures that every tiny detail is sharp and clear, which is essential when working on intricate designs or high-resolution projects.

macOS   Features   for   Graphic   Design

macOS provides a range of tools and applications that integrate seamlessly with graphic design workflows. The MacBook Air M4 supports professional design apps like Adobe Creative Cloud and Sketch. The system runs smoothly, even when running multiple apps at once or working with very large files.

- **Metal Graphics API**: As with video editing, the Metal framework benefits graphic designers by optimizing the rendering performance of design applications. This allows designers to work on heavy files, apply complex filters, and render 3D models without experiencing performance slowdowns.

- **Preview and Markup Tools**: macOS offers powerful **Preview** and **Markup** tools that let designers quickly review and edit their projects without having to open full design software. Whether you're adjusting PDF documents, adding annotations to client drafts, or making quick tweaks to vector files, these tools are both quick and intuitive.

- **External Display Support**: For professionals who need a larger workspace, the MacBook Air M4 supports multiple external displays. This is particularly useful for designers who want to work with multiple tools, reference images, or keep client feedback open while continuing to work on the main project. The MacBook Air M4 supports displays with **up to 6K resolution**, offering crystal-clear images on external monitors, perfect for designing on a larger screen.

4. Multitasking and Efficiency: Handling Multiple Professional Apps Simultaneously

One of the key advantages of the MacBook Air M4 for professionals is its ability to manage multiple demanding applications at once, thanks to the M4 chip's **unified memory architecture**. Whether you're coding while keeping a video editing timeline open or hopping between design tools and web browsers, the MacBook Air M4 handles these tasks with ease. The unified memory allows apps to share resources, leading to smoother transitions and faster app launches without consuming excessive battery or system resources.

- **Mission Control**: For multitaskers, **Mission Control** in macOS is a lifesaver. It allows you to quickly switch between multiple open windows and desktops, keeping your workspace organized and efficient. For professionals who often switch between different tasks, Mission Control is essential for maintaining focus and productivity.

- **Virtual Desktops and Split View**: Virtual desktops allow professionals to create a separate workspace for each task, reducing clutter and improving focus. You can use **Split View** to keep two apps side by side, which is incredibly useful when you need to reference one document or web page while working on another.

CHAPTER 6: PERFORMANCE OPTIMIZATION

Understanding the M4 Chip's Capabilities

The heart of the MacBook Air M4 is the newly introduced M4 chip, which is a game-changer for anyone who relies on their laptop for everyday tasks, creative work, or even more demanding professional applications. Unlike its predecessors, the M4 chip is designed to deliver unprecedented speed, efficiency, and power, all while maintaining the sleek and fanless design that MacBook Air users love.

Let's take a deeper look at how the M4 chip works its magic and why it stands out in the world of laptop processors.

1. The Architecture Behind the M4 Chip: A Look Under the Hood

The M4 chip is a custom-designed ARM-based processor developed by Apple. It integrates multiple components — CPU, GPU, Neural Engine, and unified memory — into a single chip, making it incredibly efficient and powerful. Here's a breakdown of the core components:

- **CPU (Central Processing Unit)**: The M4 features a powerful multi-core CPU that delivers a massive boost in performance compared to its predecessor, the M1. It uses a combination of high-performance cores (for demanding tasks like gaming or video editing) and high-efficiency cores (for less intensive tasks such as browsing or emailing). This design helps the MacBook Air M4 balance power and battery life effortlessly.

- **GPU (Graphics Processing Unit)**: The integrated GPU in the M4 chip is built to handle high-performance graphics tasks such as gaming, video editing, and 3D rendering. Apple has improved the GPU architecture in the M4, making it faster and more capable than the previous generation, especially in tasks that require rendering complex visuals.

- **Neural Engine**: One of the standout features of the M4 chip is its Neural Engine. This specialized processor is designed to accelerate machine learning tasks, such as image recognition, natural language processing, and augmented reality applications. If you're into AI-based apps or use tools that rely on machine learning, the M4 chip will give you a noticeable performance boost.

- **Unified Memory**: Unlike traditional computer systems that use separate memory for the CPU, GPU, and other components, the M4 chip uses unified memory. This means the CPU and GPU share the same memory pool, which leads to faster data access and improves overall system performance. Whether you're editing a high-resolution video or running multiple apps simultaneously, the M4 chip's memory management ensures everything runs smoothly.

2. Performance Benchmarks: Why the M4 Chip is a Powerhouse

Apple has designed the M4 chip with real-world performance in mind, and the numbers back it up. In terms of raw processing power, the M4 chip leaves previous generations in the dust.

- **Faster CPU Performance**: The M4 chip boasts up to 30% faster CPU performance compared to the M1 chip. Whether you're compiling code, multitasking, or running demanding applications, the M4 chip handles it all with ease. This performance improvement is particularly noticeable when you're working with larger datasets or running software that requires intense computational power.

- **Graphics Performance**: The GPU in the M4 chip has been redesigned to provide up to 40% better graphics performance than the M1. If you're into gaming or content creation, you'll appreciate how the M4 can run graphically intensive tasks without a hitch. For example, video editors can expect smoother playback and faster rendering times in apps like Final Cut Pro, while gamers can enjoy more immersive experiences in high-resolution games.

- **Machine Learning and AI**: The Neural Engine has seen a significant performance boost as well, providing up to 50% faster processing for machine learning tasks. This means that AI-based applications will run faster, and tasks like object detection or facial recognition will be more efficient.

- **Battery Efficiency**: Despite all these improvements, the M4 chip is designed to be incredibly power-efficient. Apple claims that the M4 chip is up to 50% more energy-efficient than previous Intel-based MacBook models. As a result, you get all this performance without sacrificing battery life. On a single charge, the MacBook Air M4 can easily last all day, whether you're working, streaming, or browsing.

3. Comparison to Previous Models: How the M4 Stands Out

To truly understand the significance of the M4 chip, let's compare it to the previous generations, including the M1 and Intel-based MacBook Air models.

- **M1 Chip vs. M4 Chip**: The M1 chip, introduced in 2020, was a massive leap forward for Apple, offering incredible performance and efficiency in a fanless design. But the M4 takes things even further. The M4 chip is about 30% faster than the M1 in terms of CPU performance, making it even better at handling complex workflows, multitasking, and heavy applications. Its GPU is up to 40% faster, which is a huge improvement for anyone into gaming or video editing. So, if you're using an M1 MacBook Air and considering an upgrade, the M4 will provide you with a noticeable performance boost, especially in graphics-heavy tasks.

- **Intel-based MacBook Air vs. M4 Chip**: Prior to the M1 chip, MacBook Airs were powered by Intel processors. While Intel chips offered solid performance, they couldn't match the efficiency of Apple's custom-designed silicon. The shift from Intel to the M1 (and now the M4) was revolutionary. The M4 chip offers up to 3x the CPU performance and 5x the GPU performance compared to Intel-based MacBook Airs. That means faster performance in everything from office tasks to more demanding creative projects. Plus, with the M4 chip's energy efficiency, you can expect all-day battery life, which was a challenge for Intel-powered Macs.

4. The M4 Chip vs. Competitors: How Apple Stands Out

When it comes to performance, the M4 chip doesn't just outshine its predecessors; it also sets a new bar for laptops in general. Let's compare the M4 with some of its competitors in the laptop market.

- **Apple M4 vs. Intel Core i7 (11th Gen)**: The Intel Core i7 chip is a solid performer, found in many high-end laptops, but it can't keep up with the M4's efficiency and integrated design. The M4 chip offers faster CPU performance, better energy efficiency, and superior graphics performance, all while running cooler and quieter. Intel's chips, on the other hand, require a fan to keep the laptop cool, which makes the MacBook Air M4's fanless design a major advantage.

- **Apple M4 vs. AMD Ryzen 7**: AMD's Ryzen 7 series has been praised for its multi-core performance, especially in gaming and content creation. However, the M4 chip outperforms the Ryzen 7 in single-core performance, thanks to its optimized architecture. Additionally, the M4 chip's integrated GPU is far superior, making it a better choice for graphics-heavy applications. AMD's chips also can't match the battery life of the M4, with Apple claiming up to 20 hours of video playback on a single charge, something that Ryzen-powered laptops can't compete with.

- **Apple M4 vs. Qualcomm Snapdragon 8cx Gen 3**: Qualcomm's Snapdragon processors are often used in Windows-based laptops, especially in ultra-portable models. While Snapdragon chips offer great battery life, they fall short in terms of overall performance compared to the M4 chip. The M4's CPU and GPU are more powerful, offering a more fluid experience when running demanding apps or multitasking. Plus, Apple's integration of its Neural Engine makes it a more future-proof choice for AI-based applications.

5. Why the M4 Chip is a Game-Changer

What makes the M4 chip so special isn't just the raw power it delivers, but the seamless integration of all its components into a single chip. Apple's design philosophy revolves around creating a system that works as a whole, rather than just slapping together separate parts. The M4 chip combines CPU, GPU, Neural Engine, and memory into one unified architecture, making it faster, more efficient, and more reliable than anything else on the market.

Additionally, the M4 chip's ability to deliver outstanding performance while maintaining incredible battery life is a huge advantage for anyone who values portability and efficiency. Whether you're working on the go, watching movies, or editing videos, the M4 chip ensures that your MacBook Air M4 will handle it with ease, all day long.

In short, the M4 chip is not just an upgrade; it's a game-changer that sets a new standard for performance in thin, lightweight laptops. If you're looking for a machine that can handle anything you throw at it, from casual tasks to professional-grade applications, the MacBook Air M4 with the M4 chip is the clear choice.

How to Maximize Battery Life on Your MacBook Air M4

Your MacBook Air M4 is designed to be portable and efficient, and one of its standout features is its impressive battery life. However, no matter how efficient the battery is, its longevity depends on how you use and maintain it. Whether you're working on-the-go, streaming your favorite content, or tackling a hefty project, optimizing your MacBook's battery life ensures that it will last as long as possible throughout your day.

In this section, we'll dive into practical tips and tricks that will help you maximize the battery life on your MacBook Air M4, ensuring it keeps up with you wherever you go. Let's explore how you can make the most of this amazing feature.

1. Adjust Your Screen Brightness

Your MacBook's display is one of the most power-hungry components of the device. The brighter the screen, the more battery it consumes. Fortunately, managing your screen brightness can help you extend your battery life without compromising too much on your visual experience.

- **Manual Adjustment**: You can adjust the screen brightness manually by using the **F1** (decrease) and **F2** (increase) keys on your keyboard. Experiment with different brightness levels to find a balance that works for you, but remember, the lower the brightness, the less power your MacBook needs.

- **Automatic Brightness Adjustment**: macOS comes with a built-in feature called **True Tone** and **Automatic Brightness**, which adjusts the brightness of your screen based on ambient light. To enable this feature, go to **System Preferences** > **Displays** and check the option for "Automatically adjust brightness." This can help save battery when you're in dimly lit environments.

While the MacBook Air M4's display is stunning, reducing the brightness slightly can result in noticeable battery savings, especially if you're working in a dimly lit room.

2. Enable Battery Saver (Low Power Mode)

Low Power Mode is one of the easiest ways to extend your battery life when you're running low. This feature reduces the overall energy consumption of your MacBook by limiting background activities and certain processes, including screen brightness, animations, and network activity.

To enable **Low Power Mode**, follow these steps:

1. Open **System Preferences**.

MACBOOK AIR M4 USER GUIDE

2. Click on **Battery**.

3. Select **Low Power Mode** from the left-hand side and turn it on.

When activated, Low Power Mode temporarily reduces the power used by your MacBook Air M4, allowing it to last longer, especially when you're on the go or don't have easy access to a charger.

3. Manage Your Apps and Background Processes

One of the key things you can do to preserve your battery life is to keep track of what's running in the background. Apps and processes running unnecessarily can drain your battery much faster than you think.

- **Close Unused Apps**: Make sure to close any apps you're not actively using. Open apps continue to consume resources, and even if they're in the background, they still affect your battery life. You can use the **Command + Q** shortcut to quickly quit apps, or right-click on apps in the **Dock** and choose "Quit."

- **Check Activity Monitor**: If you suspect that something is using an excessive amount of energy, go to **Applications** > **Utilities** > **Activity Monitor**. Here, you can see all running processes and their energy usage. Look for apps marked with a **"high energy impact"** tag. If you don't need them, close them to save power.

- **Limit Startup Items**: Some apps start automatically when you turn on your MacBook. This can add unnecessary load on the system and drain battery life. To control these, go to **System Preferences** > **Users**

& Groups > **Login Items**, and uncheck any apps you don't need to launch on startup.

4. Optimize Energy Settings

macOS allows you to tweak some system settings to make your MacBook Air M4 more energy-efficient. These settings can help reduce the amount of power used during idle times or when you're not actively using your laptop.

- **Energy Saver Settings**: Go to **System Preferences** > **Battery**, and you'll find options that control how your MacBook behaves when it's not in use. Adjust the **Turn display off after** slider to a shorter time if you don't mind your screen turning off when idle. This can save significant battery power.

- **Disable Visual Effects**: macOS has many visual effects that look great but can consume extra power. You can reduce the use of these effects by going to **System Preferences** > **Accessibility**, selecting **Display**, and checking **Reduce motion** and **Reduce transparency**. These adjustments won't affect your productivity but can help your MacBook last longer on a charge.

- **Power Nap**: macOS has a feature called Power Nap, which allows your MacBook to perform background tasks like checking for emails and updates while it's asleep. However, this feature can drain the battery if you're not careful. To disable it, go to **System Preferences** > **Battery** > **Power Adapter** and uncheck the **Enable Power Nap** option.

5. Turn Off Bluetooth and Wi-Fi When Not in Use

Both **Bluetooth** and **Wi-Fi** can consume battery when left on, even if you're not actively using them. If you don't need them, turning them off can help extend battery life.

- **Turn Off Bluetooth**: Go to the **Bluetooth** icon in the menu bar and click **Turn Bluetooth Off** if you're not using any Bluetooth devices.

- **Turn Off Wi-Fi**: If you're working offline or in a location where Wi-Fi isn't necessary, turn off Wi-Fi by clicking on the **Wi-Fi** icon in the menu bar and selecting **Turn Wi-Fi Off**.

It's simple but effective: switching off these connections when you don't need them can save valuable battery power.

6. Avoid Running Power-Hungry Apps

Certain apps, such as video streaming services, high-resolution games, and video editing software, are known for draining the battery quickly. While these apps may be essential for your work or leisure, consider the following strategies to extend your battery life while using them:

- **Adjust Video Quality**: When streaming videos or watching movies, reduce the video quality. For instance, in apps like YouTube, Netflix, or other streaming services, lower the resolution (e.g., from 1080p to 720p) to reduce power consumption.

- **Optimize Software Settings**: Many power-hungry apps, like photo or video editors, allow you to adjust performance settings. Reduce features like background rendering or video playback resolution, or use a simplified version of the app to save energy.

7. Use the Battery Health Management Feature

The **Battery Health Management** feature is designed to extend the overall lifespan of your MacBook's battery by reducing the peak charge when the battery is plugged in for extended periods. This is particularly useful for users who tend to keep their MacBook plugged into a charger.

To enable or check this feature:

1. Go to **System Preferences > Battery**.

2. Select **Battery Health...**.

3. Make sure **Battery health management** is enabled.

This will help preserve the longevity of your battery, ensuring that it stays healthy for a longer period and doesn't degrade as quickly over time.

8. Keep Your MacBook Air M4 Cool

Heat is another factor that can drain your battery life. When your MacBook gets too hot, it works harder, consuming more energy. Make sure to:

- **Use your MacBook on hard, flat surfaces**: Avoid using it on soft materials like beds or couches that could block airflow.

- **Ensure proper ventilation**: Keep your environment cool to prevent your MacBook from overheating.

- **Close heavy apps**: Monitor apps with high CPU usage and close them to prevent excess heat generation.

9. Monitor Battery Health Regularly

To make sure your battery stays in top shape, it's important to monitor its health over time. You can check the status of your MacBook Air M4's battery by clicking the **Apple Menu** > **About This Mac** > **System Report** > **Power**. Look for the **Cycle Count** and **Condition** under the battery information.

A healthy MacBook Air M4 battery should show "Normal" in the condition. If it shows "Replace Soon" or "Service Battery," it may be time to consider battery maintenance or replacement.

Speeding Up Your MacBook Air M4: Tips and Tools

Your MacBook Air M4 is designed to be fast, efficient, and capable of handling most tasks with ease. However, over time, like any device, it might slow down due to various reasons—whether it's an overload of unnecessary files, apps running in the background, or too many startup items. Fortunately, there are several simple and effective ways to optimize your MacBook Air M4's performance and keep it running as smoothly as the day you first unboxed it.

Let's dive into some easy-to-follow steps you can take to speed up your MacBook Air M4, ensuring you get the best experience every time you use it.

1. Clear Cache and Temporary Files

Just like a cluttered desk can make it hard to focus, a cluttered system can slow down your MacBook. Over time, your Mac accumulates cache files—temporary data stored by apps and websites to load things faster. While these files are meant to help, they can also pile up and use up precious storage space.

Here's how to clear cache and temporary files:

- **System Cache**:

  - Open **Finder** and click on **Go** in the top menu.

  - Hold down the **Option** key to reveal the **Library** option in the dropdown, then select **Library**.

  - In the Library folder, navigate to **Caches** and find the cache folders associated with apps that you use frequently (like Safari, Chrome, or Mail). You can delete these folders to free up space.

- **Browser Cache**:

  - In Safari, go to **Safari** > **Preferences** > **Advanced** and check the box next to "Show Develop menu in menu bar."

- o In the **Develop** menu, select **Empty Caches** to remove browsing data.

- o For Chrome or other browsers, you can do the same by accessing the settings and clearing the cache in the privacy section.

Regularly clearing your cache helps keep things running smoothly by freeing up storage and preventing slowdowns caused by old data.

2. Optimize Startup Items

We all love that "new laptop" feeling where everything starts up in seconds. But as you install more apps, some of them sneak their way into your **Startup Items**—meaning they automatically open when you power on your Mac. While this can be convenient for apps you use often, it can slow down your MacBook Air M4's startup time.

Here's how to remove unnecessary startup items:

- **Manage Startup Items**:

  - o Open **System Preferences** from the Apple menu in the top-left corner.

  - o Click on **Users & Groups**.

  - o Select your user account, then click the **Login Items** tab.

- Here, you'll see a list of apps that open automatically when you start your Mac. Simply select an app you don't need running right away and click the minus (-) button to remove it.

Only keep essential apps in your startup list. By reducing the number of apps that launch at startup, you can speed up the boot time and reduce unnecessary background activity.

3. Reboot Your MacBook Regularly

It might sound basic, but restarting your MacBook can sometimes do wonders for its performance. When you use your Mac for extended periods without restarting, temporary files and processes can accumulate, causing your system to slow down.

- **Simple Reboot**:

  - Go to the Apple menu and select **Restart**.

Restarting your MacBook clears memory and closes processes that might be bogging it down, giving your device a fresh start.

4. Free Up Storage Space

If your MacBook Air M4's hard drive is getting full, this can seriously impact its performance. macOS uses available storage as virtual memory, and when the drive is full, your MacBook has to work harder to manage data.

Here's how to free up space:

- **Manage Storage**:

- Click on the **Apple menu** > **About This Mac** > **Storage** tab.

- macOS will show you a breakdown of your storage usage, including documents, apps, and system files. You can use the **Manage** button to see options for optimizing storage.

- **Delete Unnecessary Files**:

  - Remove old downloads, duplicates, and files you no longer need. You can also delete apps you don't use or transfer large files to an external hard drive or cloud storage (iCloud, Google Drive, etc.).

A little decluttering goes a long way. The more space you free up, the faster your MacBook can access the data it needs to run apps and processes.

5. Use Disk Utility to Repair Disk Permissions

Disk permissions are settings that determine who can read or modify files on your Mac. Sometimes, these settings can get corrupted, which may slow down your MacBook's performance.

Here's how to use **Disk Utility** to repair permissions:

- **Run Disk Utility**:

  - Open **Finder** > **Applications** > **Utilities** and launch **Disk Utility**.

  - In Disk Utility, select your main disk (usually called **Macintosh HD**) from the sidebar.

o   Click on **First Aid** and then click **Run**. This will check the disk for errors and repair any damaged or corrupted files, potentially improving performance.

Running **First Aid** helps maintain the integrity of your system, preventing minor issues from escalating into bigger problems.

6. Remove Unnecessary Apps and Extensions

Over time, you may have accumulated apps and browser extensions that you no longer use. These can consume resources and slow down your MacBook Air M4.

- **Remove Unwanted Apps**:

  o   Open **Finder** and go to **Applications**.

  o   Drag apps you no longer use to the Trash.

- **Delete Unused Browser Extensions**:

  o   In Safari, go to **Safari** > **Preferences** > **Extensions**, and remove any extensions you no longer need.

  o   For Chrome or Firefox, you can manage extensions in their respective settings menus.

By keeping only the apps and extensions that are essential to your daily workflow, you can improve overall system performance.

7. Keep macOS and Apps Up to Date

Keeping your MacBook's operating system and apps up to date ensures that you have the latest features, bug fixes, and performance improvements.

- **Update macOS**:

  - o Go to **System Preferences** > **Software Update**.

  - o If an update is available, click **Update Now**.

- **Update Apps**:

  - o Open the **App Store** and go to the **Updates** tab to check for app updates.

  - o Alternatively, you can enable automatic updates for apps in **System Preferences** > **App Store**.

Regular updates often contain optimizations that can boost performance, improve security, and ensure everything runs as efficiently as possible.

8. Reset the SMC (System Management Controller)

Sometimes, resetting the SMC can help with various performance issues, particularly those related to power management, battery, and thermal management. If you've noticed your MacBook Air M4 running hotter than usual or its battery draining quickly, resetting the SMC might help.

- **How to Reset the SMC**:

  1. Shut down your MacBook.

2. Hold **Shift** + **Control** + **Option** (on the left side of your keyboard) and press the **Power** button simultaneously for 10 seconds.

3. Release all keys, then press the **Power** button to turn your MacBook back on.

Resetting the SMC can help resolve issues that may be affecting your Mac's power efficiency and overall performance.

Monitoring System Performance with Activity Monitor

In this section, we will dive into one of the most essential tools for MacBook users: **Activity Monitor**. It's like the control center for your Mac, where you can keep an eye on how your system is performing, troubleshoot slowdowns, and ensure that everything is running smoothly. Whether you're a newbie or a seasoned user, understanding how to use Activity Monitor effectively can make a world of difference in your MacBook Air M4's performance.

What is Activity Monitor?

Activity Monitor is a built-in macOS utility that shows you a real-time overview of all the processes running on your Mac. It helps you see how much CPU, memory, disk, and network resources are being used by different apps and processes. It's an indispensable tool for diagnosing issues like slowdowns, unresponsive apps, or excessive battery drain.

Where to Find Activity Monitor:

To open Activity Monitor, follow these simple steps:

1. **Using Spotlight**: Press Command + Space to open Spotlight Search. Type "Activity Monitor" and press Return.

2. **Via Applications**: Open the Finder, click on the **Applications** folder, then go to **Utilities** and double-click on **Activity Monitor**.

Once open, you'll be greeted with a series of tabs and data that help you monitor various aspects of your system's performance.

Understanding the Activity Monitor Tabs

When you open Activity Monitor, you'll see several tabs at the top of the window: **CPU**, **Memory**, **Energy**, **Disk**, and **Network**. Let's break down what each of these tabs does:

1. **CPU Tab**:

   o **What It Tracks**: This tab shows how much processing power (CPU usage) each app or process is using. It's crucial for identifying which applications are using up too much of your CPU, leading to potential system slowdowns.

MACBOOK AIR M4 USER GUIDE

- o **What to Look For**: If you notice that a specific app or process is taking up a large chunk of your CPU usage, it could be the reason why your Mac is lagging or getting hot.

- o **Troubleshooting Tip**: If an app is consuming too much CPU, try quitting it (highlight the app, click the X button, or press Command + Q in the app). If this doesn't work, you may need to force quit the app by clicking the X button in Activity Monitor.

2. **Memory Tab**:

   - o **What It Tracks**: This tab displays how much RAM (memory) is being used by each process. If you find that your MacBook is running slowly or freezing, it could be because too many apps or processes are using too much memory.

   - o **What to Look For**: If the **Memory Pressure** graph is in the **green** zone, everything is good. However, if it's **yellow** or **red**, it means your system is struggling to handle the load, and apps might start to crash or slow down.

   - o **Troubleshooting Tip**: Close apps that you aren't using. If the issue persists, consider restarting your Mac to refresh the memory and clear any unnecessary processes.

3. **Energy Tab**:

   o **What It Tracks**: The Energy tab shows how much energy each app and process is using, which is particularly useful if you're trying to conserve battery life.

   o **What to Look For**: Check for apps that are consuming high amounts of energy. This is important if you're noticing fast battery drain.

   o **Troubleshooting Tip**: If you're trying to save battery life, consider quitting apps with high energy usage or switching to more energy-efficient alternatives.

4. **Disk Tab**:

   o **What It Tracks**: This tab shows you how much data is being read from and written to your disk. It's helpful for tracking down processes that are using up disk space or causing slowdowns due to excessive disk activity.

   o **What to Look For**: Look for apps that are writing or reading large amounts of data. If your disk usage is constantly high, it could lead to slower performance, especially if you have limited disk space.

   o **Troubleshooting Tip**: If you notice heavy disk usage, check if large files are being processed in the background (like backups, downloads, or updates). Consider closing apps that are engaging in unnecessary disk activity.

5. **Network Tab**:

   o **What It Tracks**: The Network tab shows how much data is being sent and received by your MacBook. This is important if you're noticing slow internet speeds or network-related performance issues.

   o **What to Look For**: If a particular app or process is consuming too much network bandwidth, it could be slowing down your internet connection or draining your battery.

   o **Troubleshooting Tip**: If you're experiencing slow internet, check for apps that are using your network heavily, such as cloud backup services or streaming apps. You can either pause or adjust these apps' settings to reduce their bandwidth usage.

Identifying Resource-Hogging Apps

One of the primary uses of Activity Monitor is to identify which apps are consuming the most resources, causing slowdowns, or draining your battery faster than usual. Here's how you can identify and handle resource-hogging apps:

1. **Look at CPU and Memory Usage**: If an app is using an unusually high amount of CPU or memory, it's a clear indicator that it's likely contributing to your system's slowdown.

   o **High CPU Usage**: If an app is constantly using a large percentage of the CPU (e.g., 70% or higher), it's putting unnecessary stress on your system. Consider quitting the app or checking for any available updates that may fix performance issues.

- o **High Memory Usage**: Similarly, if an app is using up a lot of memory (especially if it's above 4GB in some cases), it might be causing your system to lag. You may need to restart your Mac or uninstall unnecessary apps.

2. **Check for Background Processes**: Some apps run background processes that consume system resources. For example, cloud-sync apps like Dropbox, Google Drive, or OneDrive constantly sync files and may put a strain on both your CPU and memory. You can disable or pause syncing temporarily to reduce their load.

3. **Close Unused Apps**: One of the simplest ways to free up resources is to close apps that you're not actively using. Keep Activity Monitor open so you can monitor your system's resource usage while you work.

Troubleshooting Slowdowns and Improving Performance

If you're noticing that your MacBook Air M4 is running slower than usual, here are some steps to troubleshoot the issue:

1. **Force Quit Unresponsive Apps**: If an app becomes unresponsive or frozen, you can force quit it from Activity Monitor. This will free up system resources and allow your Mac to return to normal functioning.

   - o To force quit an app, select it in Activity Monitor, click on the **X** button in the top-left corner, and choose **Force Quit**.

2. **Restart Your Mac**: Restarting your Mac can help clear out any processes that are stuck or using too many resources. This can be especially helpful if your MacBook has been running for an extended period without a restart.

3. **Clear Cache Files**: Cache files can sometimes take up a lot of space and slow down your system. Consider using macOS's built-in tools or third-party apps like CleanMyMac to clear these files and free up space.

4. **Update Software**: Always keep your macOS and apps updated. Sometimes, performance issues are the result of bugs or inefficiencies in older versions of software. Activity Monitor can even show you if any processes are running older versions of apps that need updates.

5. **Check Disk Space**: Running low on disk space can cause your MacBook Air M4 to slow down. If you notice that disk usage is high, it might be time to delete old files or move them to an external hard drive or cloud storage. Activity Monitor's **Disk** tab can help you identify apps that are using excessive disk space.

CHAPTER 7: TROUBLESHOOTING AND FAQS

Common Issues and How to Fix Them

Every MacBook Air M4 user, no matter how experienced, will encounter some challenges from time to time. Whether you're having trouble with Wi-Fi, dealing with freezing apps, or facing slow system performance, understanding how to troubleshoot and resolve these issues is crucial to maintaining an optimal experience with your MacBook. Below are some common issues you might run into and practical, easy-to-follow steps to fix them.

1. Wi-Fi Issues: "Why Can't I Connect?"

Wi-Fi problems are among the most common headaches for MacBook users. Whether your MacBook Air M4 won't connect to Wi-Fi, keeps disconnecting, or has a slow internet speed, here's what you can do to solve the problem:

Issue: MacBook Won't Connect to Wi-Fi

This is one of the most frustrating issues, but the fix is usually simple.

Solution:

1. **Check if Wi-Fi is On**: The first thing you should check is whether your Wi-Fi is enabled on the MacBook. Go to the **Wi-Fi icon** in the top-right corner of the menu bar and ensure it's turned on.

2. **Restart Your Mac**: Sometimes, a quick restart is all it takes. Click on the **Apple logo** and select **Restart**. Once your Mac restarts, try reconnecting to the Wi-Fi.

3. **Forget and Reconnect**:

   o Go to **System Preferences** > **Network** > **Wi-Fi** > **Advanced**.

   o From the list of saved networks, find your network, click on it, and then click **Remove**.

   o After that, reconnect to your Wi-Fi network by selecting it from the Wi-Fi list and entering the password.

4. **Check Router Settings**: Sometimes, the problem lies with your router. Try rebooting it by unplugging it for 10-20 seconds, then plugging it back in. Check if other devices are having trouble connecting. If not, it's likely a MacBook-specific issue.

5. **Reset Your Network Settings**:

   o Open **System Preferences** > **Network** > **Wi-Fi**.

   o Click on **Advanced**, then click **Reset**.

o   This will reset your Wi-Fi settings, clearing out any potential errors that might be preventing the connection.

Issue: Slow Wi-Fi Connection

If your MacBook is connected but the internet is crawling, it can be especially frustrating when you need to get work done or stream videos.

Solution:

1. **Move Closer to the Router**: Physical obstructions like walls or furniture can impact the Wi-Fi signal strength. If possible, try moving your MacBook closer to your router.

2. **Check Internet Speed**: Sometimes the issue isn't your MacBook, but your internet speed. You can use a site like Speedtest.net to check your internet speed. If the results are lower than expected, contact your internet service provider (ISP) for assistance.

3. **Use a 5GHz Network**: If your router supports both 2.4GHz and 5GHz Wi-Fi bands, try switching to the 5GHz network. It's typically faster and less prone to interference from other devices.

4. **Close Background Apps**: If there are apps running in the background using your bandwidth, it can slow down your internet speed. Go to **Activity Monitor** (under **Applications > Utilities**) and close any apps using excessive resources.

5. **Clear DNS Cache**: Sometimes clearing the DNS cache can help speed up your connection:

- Open **Terminal** (find it in **Applications > Utilities**).

- Type the following command and press Enter:

"sudo killall -HUP mDNSResponder"

- This will flush your DNS cache and can improve internet speeds.

2. MacBook Air M4 Freezing: "Everything's Stuck!"

At some point, you might find that your MacBook Air M4 starts freezing—apps become unresponsive, or your system starts to lag badly. Don't panic! This is a common issue that can usually be resolved with a few troubleshooting steps.

Issue: MacBook Freezing or Becoming Unresponsive

Solution:

1. **Force Quit the Application**: When an app freezes, the first step is to force quit it. You can do this by:

   - Press **Command + Option + Esc** to bring up the **Force Quit Applications** window.

   - Select the frozen app and click **Force Quit**.

2. **Close Unnecessary Apps**: Running too many apps at once can cause your MacBook to freeze. Close any apps you're not currently using:

- o Go to the **Dock**, right-click on the app, and choose **Quit**.

- o Or, press **Command + Q** to quickly close apps.

3. **Restart Your Mac**: If the freezing continues, try restarting your MacBook. Hold down the **Power button** for a few seconds to force a shutdown, then restart it.

4. **Check for Software Updates**: Sometimes, freezing can be caused by bugs in macOS that are fixed in newer updates. Go to **System Preferences** > **Software Update** and install any available updates.

5. **Check for Malware or System Corruption**: While macOS is generally secure, it's possible to encounter malware or corrupted system files. Run a disk check using the **Disk Utility** tool:

- o Open **Disk Utility** (find it in **Applications > Utilities**).

- o Select your main hard drive (usually labeled "Macintosh HD") and click **First Aid**.

- o This tool will scan and repair any file system errors that could be causing the freezing.

3. App Crashes: "Why Is My App Closing Unexpectedly?"

App crashes are another common issue. Whether it's a productivity app like Word or a video streaming app like Netflix, crashes can disrupt your workflow and waste your time. Here's how to fix it.

Issue: Apps Keep Crashing

Solution:

1. **Update the App**: Check the App Store to see if there's an update for the app causing the crashes. Developers often release bug fixes that can solve stability issues.

2. **Reinstall the App**:

   o If an app continues to crash despite updates, try reinstalling it.

   o Go to the **Applications folder**, drag the app to the **Trash**, and then download and reinstall it from the **App Store** or the developer's website.

3. **Clear App Cache**: Some apps store temporary files that can become corrupted, causing crashes. You can clear the app's cache by:

   o Opening **Finder**.

   o Pressing **Shift + Command + G** and typing ~/Library/Caches.

   o Find the folder for the app causing issues, delete its contents, and restart the app.

4. **Check Console Logs for Errors**: If an app consistently crashes, it may be helpful to check the system logs to see what's going wrong:

   o Open **Console** (in **Applications > Utilities**).

   o Look for any recent error messages related to the app and take note of the error codes. You can then search for these error codes online for a specific fix.

5. **Create a New User Account**: Sometimes, user-specific settings or files cause app crashes. Create a new user account and test if the app works under that account:

   o Go to **System Preferences** > **Users & Groups** and click the + to add a new account.

   o Log into the new account and try running the app again.

4. MacBook Running Slow: "Why Is My MacBook So Slow?"

A slow MacBook can be frustrating, especially when you need to get work done or enjoy a smooth multimedia experience. Here's how to speed things up:

Issue: MacBook Slowing Down Over Time

Solution:

1. **Free Up Disk Space**: If your hard drive is nearly full, it can slow down your Mac. Check how much space you have by going to **Apple Menu** > **About This Mac** > **Storage**. Remove unnecessary files or move them to an external drive or iCloud.

2. **Clear Browser Cache and History**: Browsers store a lot of data that can slow things down over time. Clear your browser's cache and history by going to the browser settings and selecting **Clear Browsing Data**.

3. **Disable Startup Items**: Some apps automatically start when you turn on your MacBook, which can slow it down. To disable unnecessary startup items:

    o Go to **System Preferences** > **Users & Groups** > **Login Items**.

    o Remove any apps that you don't need to start automatically.

4. **Run Disk Cleanup**: Open **Disk Utility**, select your hard drive, and click on **First Aid** to repair any disk issues that could be affecting performance.

5. **Upgrade RAM**: If you're running demanding apps or multitasking a lot, your Mac may need more RAM. While the RAM in the MacBook Air M4 isn't upgradeable after purchase, consider choosing a higher RAM configuration if you're getting a new MacBook.

5. Bluetooth Connectivity Issues: "Why Won't My Bluetooth Devices Connect?"

If your Bluetooth accessories (like a wireless mouse, keyboard, or headphones) won't connect or are acting strangely, it can be incredibly frustrating. Here's how to fix it.

Issue: Bluetooth Not Connecting to Devices

Solution:

1. **Toggle Bluetooth Off and On**: Sometimes, simply turning Bluetooth off and back on can fix the issue. Go to **System Preferences** > **Bluetooth** and click the **Turn Bluetooth Off** button. Wait a few seconds and then turn it back on.

2. **Forget and Reconnect the Device**:

   o In the **Bluetooth** menu, right-click the device you're having trouble with and select **Remove**.

   o Then, pair the device again by putting it into pairing mode and selecting it in the Bluetooth list.

3. **Restart Your MacBook**: Sometimes a quick restart can resolve Bluetooth connectivity issues. Restart your Mac by clicking on the **Apple logo** in the top left and selecting **Restart**.

4. **Reset the Bluetooth Module**:

   o Open **Terminal** (in **Applications** > **Utilities**).

   o Type the following command and press **Enter**:

"sudo pkill bluetoothd"

   o This will reset the Bluetooth module. After doing this, try connecting your device again.

5. **Update macOS**: Check if there's a software update available, as sometimes Bluetooth issues can be related to bugs that have been

fixed in newer updates. Go to **System Preferences** > **Software Update** and install any available updates.

6. MacBook Air M4 Overheating: "Why Is My Mac So Hot?"

Overheating can be a sign that your MacBook Air is working harder than usual or that there's a potential issue with its cooling system. Here's how to prevent your Mac from overheating.

Issue: MacBook Air M4 Overheating

Solution:

1. **Close Unnecessary Apps**: Running multiple apps at once can make your MacBook work harder, causing it to overheat. Close any apps you aren't actively using by going to the **Dock** and right-clicking on the app to select **Quit**.

2. **Monitor CPU Usage**: If you notice your MacBook is running hot, open **Activity Monitor** (in **Applications** > **Utilities**) and check the **CPU** tab for any apps that are consuming too many system resources. Close or force quit any resource-hogging apps.

3. **Keep Your MacBook on a Hard, Flat Surface**: Avoid using your MacBook on soft surfaces like a bed or couch, as this can block the airflow and cause it to overheat. Place your Mac on a flat, hard surface to ensure it stays cool.

4. **Clean the Vents**: Over time, dust can accumulate inside your MacBook's vents, blocking airflow. Use compressed air to gently clean the vents. Make sure the MacBook is off before doing this to avoid causing damage.

5. **Use Activity Monitor to Check for Background Processes**: Open **Activity Monitor**, check the **Energy** tab, and disable any background processes that could be causing unnecessary heat.

6. **Use an External Cooling Pad**: If you're using your MacBook for intensive tasks like gaming or video editing, consider purchasing an external cooling pad to help regulate temperature.

7. MacBook Air M4 Slow Startup: "Why Is My Mac Taking So Long to Boot?"

If you notice that your MacBook Air M4 is taking longer than usual to start up, it might be due to a number of factors. Here's how to speed up the startup process.

Issue: Slow Startup Time

Solution:

1. **Reduce Startup Programs**: Some apps automatically launch when you start your Mac, slowing down the startup process. To disable unnecessary startup items:

   o   Go to **System Preferences** > **Users & Groups** > **Login Items**.

o Remove any apps that aren't essential.

2. **Clear Out Your Startup Disk**: If your hard drive is nearly full, it can slow down the boot process. Go to **Apple Menu > About This Mac > Storage** and remove any unnecessary files. Consider moving large files, like videos or documents, to an external hard drive or iCloud.

3. **Reset the NVRAM**: NVRAM (Non-Volatile Random-Access Memory) stores certain settings, and resetting it can help with startup problems:

   o Shut down your MacBook.

   o Turn it on and immediately press and hold **Option + Command + P + R** for about 20 seconds.

   o Release the keys, and let the MacBook restart.

4. **Use Disk Utility to Repair Your Startup Disk**: Open **Disk Utility** (in **Applications > Utilities**), select your startup disk, and click **First Aid** to check for and repair any issues with the disk that could be affecting startup speed.

8. MacBook Air M4 Trackpad Not Responding: "Why Is My Trackpad Not Working?"

If your MacBook Air M4's trackpad stops responding, it can be a major inconvenience. Here's how to fix it.

Issue: Trackpad Not Responding or Acting Erratically

Solution:

1. **Restart Your Mac**: Sometimes a restart is all it takes to fix trackpad issues. If your trackpad is unresponsive, click the **Apple logo** and choose **Restart**.

2. **Check for External Devices**: If you have external devices connected to your Mac, such as a mouse or USB hub, try unplugging them to see if they're causing the issue.

3. **Update macOS**: Ensure your macOS is up-to-date, as software updates can fix trackpad-related bugs. Go to **System Preferences > Software Update** and install any available updates.

4. **Reset the SMC (System Management Controller)**: If your trackpad is still unresponsive, try resetting the SMC. To reset the SMC on a MacBook Air M4:

   o Shut down your MacBook.

   o Press and hold the **Shift + Control + Option** keys on the left side of the built-in keyboard, then press the **Power** button.

   o Hold these keys for 10 seconds, then release.

   o Press the **Power** button again to turn on your MacBook.

5. **Check Trackpad Settings**: Go to **System Preferences > Trackpad** and ensure that all trackpad settings are configured correctly. You can

adjust settings like **Tap to Click**, **Scroll Direction**, and **Secondary Click**.

6. **Test in Safe Mode**: Boot your Mac in Safe Mode by holding the **Shift** key as your Mac starts up. This will disable non-essential software, which could help diagnose whether a third-party app is causing the issue.

9. MacBook Air M4 No Sound: "Why Can't I Hear Anything?"

No sound on your MacBook Air M4 can be frustrating, especially when you're watching a video or attending a meeting. Here's how to fix it.

Issue: No Sound Coming from MacBook Air M4

Solution:

1. **Check Volume Settings**: First, make sure that your volume is turned up and not muted. Click the **Sound icon** in the menu bar and adjust the volume.

2. **Select the Correct Output Device**: If you have Bluetooth speakers or headphones connected, your Mac might be outputting sound to those devices instead of the built-in speakers. Go to **System Preferences > Sound > Output** and select **Internal Speakers**.

3. **Restart Your Mac**: Sometimes a simple restart can fix sound issues. Click on the **Apple logo** and choose **Restart**.

4. **Check for Software Updates**: Outdated software can sometimes cause sound issues. Go to **System Preferences > Software Update** to check for and install any updates.

5. **Reset the Core Audio**: Open **Terminal** (Applications > Utilities) and type the following command:

"sudo killall coreaudiod"

This will restart the audio system and may resolve any issues with sound.

6. **Check Audio Preferences**: Go to **System Preferences > Sound** and make sure that the settings are correctly configured for your device. Test the sound by playing a sample audio file to ensure that everything is working.

Solving Problems with Apps and macOS Updates

One of the great things about owning a MacBook Air M4 is the seamless experience with macOS and its apps. But like any technology, you might occasionally run into hiccups—apps freezing, updates not installing, or apps just not behaving as expected. Fortunately, troubleshooting app and macOS issues on your MacBook is usually straightforward. Let's walk through some of the most common problems users face and how you can resolve them, while also sharing best practices for keeping your software up to date.

1. Troubleshooting Apps on Your MacBook Air M4

Apps are the backbone of your MacBook's functionality, whether you're working, playing games, or creating content. But sometimes apps misbehave, crash, or refuse to open. Let's look at how you can fix these issues:

App Not Responding or Freezing

When an app freezes and becomes unresponsive, it can be frustrating. Here's how to fix it:

1. **Force Quit the App**:

   o Press **Command + Option + Escape** to bring up the Force Quit menu.

   o Select the frozen app from the list and click **Force Quit**.

   o Wait for the app to close completely, then try reopening it.

2. **Check for System Resource Usage**:

   o Open **Activity Monitor** (found in **Applications > Utilities**).

   o Look for any apps that are using excessive CPU or memory.

   o If an app is consuming too many resources, it may cause the system to freeze. You can try quitting these apps from Activity Monitor.

3. **Restart Your MacBook**:

   o Sometimes the best fix is simply restarting your Mac. Click the Apple logo in the top-left corner and select **Restart**. This can help reset system processes and clear temporary glitches.

4. **Check for App-Specific Issues**:

   o If the app continues to freeze, it might be an issue specific to that app. Try uninstalling and reinstalling the app (we'll cover this next). You can also check the app's website or support forums for known issues or updates.

2. Updating or Reinstalling Apps

It's important to keep your apps up to date to ensure they run smoothly and securely. Here's how you can update or reinstall apps on your MacBook Air M4:

Updating Apps via the Mac App Store

Many apps you install will come from the **Mac App Store**. Keeping them updated is easy:

1. Open the **App Store**.

2. Click on **Updates** in the left-hand sidebar.

3. If there are any available updates for your apps, you'll see them listed here.

4. Click **Update All** to update all apps at once or update them individually.

Updating Apps Outside the Mac App Store

For apps downloaded from websites or third-party sources, you may need to update them manually. Here's how:

1. Open the app.

2. Go to the app's **preferences** or **settings** (usually found in the app's menu bar at the top of the screen).

3. Look for an option like **Check for Updates** or **Software Update**.

4. Follow the instructions to update the app. If no update option is found, you may need to download the latest version from the developer's website.

Reinstalling an App

If an app continues to misbehave after updating, or if updating doesn't fix the problem, reinstalling might be the best option. Here's how to do it:

1. **Delete the App**:

   o Open **Finder** and go to **Applications**.

   o Find the app you want to uninstall, then either drag it to the **Trash** or right-click and select **Move to Trash**.

2. **Reinstall the App**:

    o If the app is from the **Mac App Store**, simply search for it again in the App Store and click **Install**.

    o For third-party apps, visit the developer's website or the source where you originally downloaded the app. Download the latest version and install it again.

3. Solving macOS Software Issues

macOS is the heart of your MacBook Air M4, and like any system software, it sometimes experiences issues. Below are common macOS problems and how to fix them:

System Update Problems

macOS updates are crucial for keeping your system secure and running efficiently. But what if your MacBook Air M4 refuses to update or encounters problems during an update? Here's how to resolve those issues:

1. **Ensure Enough Storage Space**:

    o If your Mac doesn't have enough storage space for the update, it may fail to install. To check:

        ▪ Go to **Apple Menu > About This Mac > Storage**.

- If your storage is almost full, you may need to free up space by deleting unused files or moving data to an external drive.

2. **Check for Internet Connection Issues**:

   o A poor internet connection can interrupt the download of the macOS update. Make sure your Wi-Fi is stable and strong.

   o You can test your connection by opening **Safari** and visiting a website to check if the internet is working properly.

3. **Restart Your MacBook**:

   o If the update is stuck, try restarting your MacBook and then attempt the update again.

4. **Update in Safe Mode**:

   o If your MacBook still won't update, try restarting in **Safe Mode**. Here's how:

   - Turn off your MacBook.

   - Turn it back on and immediately press and hold the **Shift** key.

   - Release the key when you see the login window.

   - Once in Safe Mode, try updating macOS again.

Software Not Responding After Update

Sometimes after a macOS update, apps or the system may start acting weird or stop responding entirely. Here's what to do:

1. **Reset NVRAM/PRAM**:

   o Sometimes, issues after updates can be related to system settings stored in the NVRAM/PRAM. Resetting it may fix the problem.

   o To reset it:

      ▪ Turn off your Mac.

      ▪ Turn it back on and immediately press and hold **Option + Command + P + R** for about 20 seconds.

      ▪ Release the keys and let your Mac restart.

2. **Rebuild Spotlight Index**:

   o If Spotlight is slow or unresponsive, rebuilding its index can help.

      ▪ Go to **System Preferences > Spotlight > Privacy**.

      ▪ Drag your hard drive into the list, then remove it after a few seconds to rebuild the index.

3. **Check for Third-Party Software Conflicts**:

o If you installed third-party apps or extensions before the update, one of them might be causing issues. Try uninstalling recent apps or extensions to see if that fixes the problem.

macOS Is Slow After an Update

If macOS is running slower than usual after an update, here's what you can do to speed things up:

1. **Clear Cache and Temporary Files**:

   o Open **Finder** and go to **Go > Go to Folder**.

   o Type ~/Library/Caches and press **Enter**.

   o You can delete the files inside each folder, but be cautious not to remove folders themselves. This can free up space and improve performance.

2. **Check Login Items**:

   o Some apps automatically start when you log in, and too many of these can slow down your Mac.

   o Go to **System Preferences > Users & Groups** and select your account.

   o Click the **Login Items** tab and remove unnecessary apps.

3. **Run Disk Utility**:

   o Open **Disk Utility** (Applications > Utilities) and select your hard drive.

MACBOOK AIR M4 USER GUIDE

o   Click on **First Aid** to check and repair any disk issues that may be slowing down your Mac.

4. Best Practices for Maintaining Software Updates

Keeping your MacBook Air M4 updated is one of the best ways to avoid issues and ensure optimal performance. Here are some best practices for maintaining your software:

1. **Enable Automatic Updates**:

   o   macOS can automatically download and install important updates, ensuring your system stays current with security patches and bug fixes. To enable automatic updates:

   ▪   Go to **System Preferences > Software Update**.

   ▪   Check the box for **Automatically keep my Mac up to date**.

2. **Set a Schedule for Manual Checks**:

   o   Even with automatic updates, it's a good idea to manually check for updates every few weeks. This ensures you don't miss out on minor updates that may have been delayed.

3. **Back Up Before Updating**:

   o   Before performing any major macOS update, always back up your data using **Time Machine** or another backup method.

This way, if anything goes wrong during the update, you can restore your system to its previous state.

4. **Use the macOS Recovery Mode**:

    o   If things go wrong with macOS and you're unable to boot into the system, you can always use macOS Recovery to reinstall macOS or restore from a Time Machine backup. To enter Recovery Mode:

        ▪   Turn off your Mac, then turn it on while holding **Command + R**.

When to Contact Apple Support: Troubleshooting Resources

While your MacBook Air M4 is designed to be user-friendly and reliable, there may be times when you encounter issues that require a bit more assistance than a quick Google search or a troubleshooting step can fix. In these cases, it's important to know when and how to reach out to Apple Support for help. Whether you're dealing with hardware problems, complex software glitches, or any issue that's just a little too tricky, Apple has multiple ways to offer guidance.

Let's walk through when it's time to contact Apple Support and the steps to do so efficiently, ensuring you get the help you need without unnecessary stress.

When to Contact Apple Support

First, let's talk about when it's appropriate to get in touch with Apple Support. While many common issues can be resolved with a little patience or a few troubleshooting steps, some problems may require more expert help. Here are a few scenarios where contacting Apple Support might be your best course of action:

1. **Persistent Software Issues**: If your MacBook Air M4 is constantly freezing, crashing, or showing error messages that won't go away despite restarting your MacBook or reinstalling macOS, it may indicate a deeper software issue. Sometimes, the problem may be related to a specific app or a macOS update that didn't go as planned. If you've tried basic solutions like updating software, resetting the PRAM/NVRAM, and running Disk Utility, but the problem persists, it's time to contact Apple Support.

2. **Hardware Problems**: Issues such as a malfunctioning keyboard, broken screen, or issues with the USB-C ports or camera (e.g., the camera not turning on, poor video quality) are prime candidates for contacting Apple. Apple technicians have the tools and expertise to run diagnostic tests to pinpoint the issue accurately. If your MacBook Air M4 is under warranty, you might also be eligible for repairs or replacements if necessary.

MACBOOK AIR M4 USER GUIDE

3. **Unresponsive or Faulty Battery**: Battery-related issues can vary from not charging properly to battery draining too quickly. While macOS offers some built-in diagnostics, it can be tricky to figure out what's really wrong with the battery without professional help. If you've tried optimizing battery settings, but it's still underperforming, Apple Support can guide you through battery management or help arrange for a replacement if needed.

4. **MacBook Air M4 Overheating**: Overheating can sometimes be the result of heavy applications running or a dusty fan, but if your MacBook is getting excessively hot even during light use, it could signal an internal issue, like a problem with the cooling system or a faulty part. Apple Support can help diagnose the issue remotely or guide you through solutions.

5. **Account and iCloud Issues**: iCloud syncing problems, Apple ID issues, and other account-related concerns can be tricky to fix on your own. For example, if you're having trouble signing in to your Apple ID, accessing your iCloud files, or syncing data between devices, Apple Support can assist in resolving account issues, from password recovery to account configuration.

6. **Peripherals Not Working**: If you're having trouble with external peripherals, like printers, displays, or external hard drives, connecting properly to your MacBook Air M4, it could be due to a software conflict or an issue with the hardware. Apple Support can troubleshoot

the issue with you and help determine if it's a compatibility problem or something that needs a software fix.

7. **System Performance Issues**: If your MacBook Air M4 is running sluggishly despite you not having many apps open, or it's suddenly unresponsive to simple tasks, it might be due to a deeper system issue like a corrupted file, bad memory, or even malware. Apple Support can help with diagnostics and solutions to improve system performance.

How to Contact Apple Support

Now that we've covered when to contact Apple Support, let's go through the process of how to get in touch with them.

Option 1: Using the Apple Help Center

The **Apple Help Center** is your first stop when you need guidance or want to troubleshoot on your own. It provides step-by-step guides, videos, and a search feature where you can type in your issue and find helpful articles.

- **Visit the Apple Help Center**: Open your browser and go to https://support.apple.com/. From there, you can search for your issue or browse through categories to find answers. Most common problems (e.g., Wi-Fi issues, battery life, macOS problems) have well-documented solutions here.

- **Browse Common Issues**: On the Help Center, you can explore various categories such as **Mac**, **iCloud**, **Apps**, and **Hardware**. If you're having trouble with your MacBook Air M4, click on the **Mac** section to get specific help. Apple's support articles often have detailed, easy-to-follow instructions that may solve your problem without needing to contact support directly.

- **Find a Step-by-Step Solution**: For issues like battery optimization, slow performance, or app errors, the Help Center provides comprehensive step-by-step guides. If a guide doesn't resolve your issue, you can proceed to live support.

Option 2: Contacting Apple Support via Phone or Chat

If the Apple Help Center didn't solve your problem, the next step is to reach out to Apple Support directly. Here's how you can do that:

- **Live Chat**: One of the fastest ways to get help is by using Apple's online chat feature. Simply visit the Apple Support page, and when prompted, choose the "Chat" option. You'll be connected to an Apple technician who will walk you through troubleshooting steps and offer solutions. This is especially useful if you need help with a specific error message or app-related issue.

- **Phone Support**: If you prefer speaking to someone on the phone, you can contact Apple Support by calling the number listed on their website. For U.S. users, the number is 1-800-APL-CARE (1-800-275-2273), but Apple has different numbers based on your region. Simply follow the prompts and you'll be connected to a support agent. This is a great option for more complex issues that might require detailed explanations or screen sharing.

- **Apple Support App**: If you're using an iPhone or iPad, you can download the **Apple Support app** from the App Store. The app gives you easy access to troubleshooting guides, appointment booking, and direct contact with Apple experts via chat or phone. The app also lets you schedule an appointment at your nearest Apple Store or Apple-authorized service provider if the issue requires in-person help.

Option 3: Apple's Online Forums

Apple's **online forums** are a great resource for getting advice from fellow Mac users. These forums are filled with helpful posts from people who have faced similar issues. If you don't want to wait for official support, browsing or posting in the forums might give you a quick solution.

- **How to Use the Apple Community Forum**: Visit the Apple Support Community at https://discussions.apple.com/. Use the search bar to see if someone else has already asked about your issue. If not, create a post detailing your problem. Be sure to include as much information as possible, such as what you've tried to fix the issue and any error messages you've seen.

- **Getting Help from Other Users**: Sometimes the best advice comes from fellow Apple users who have gone through similar situations. Whether it's tips on dealing with a specific software bug or advice on optimizing performance, the Apple Community is a wealth of knowledge. Keep in mind, though, that the advice here is not official, so it's always a good idea to double-check with Apple Support for the most accurate solutions.

Option 4: In-Person Support at Apple Stores

If the issue with your MacBook Air M4 is hardware-related or requires a physical examination, you can visit an **Apple Store** or an **Apple-authorized service provider** for in-person support.

- **Booking an Appointment**: You can schedule a Genius Bar appointment directly through the **Apple Support app** or the **Apple website**. If you need immediate assistance, you can walk into the Apple Store, but be prepared for possible wait times, especially during peak hours.

- **What to Expect at the Genius Bar**: When you arrive at your appointment, the Genius Bar technician will assess your MacBook Air M4. They'll run diagnostics, check for hardware issues, and recommend solutions. If your MacBook needs repairs, they can often do them on-site or schedule a follow-up appointment for repairs that require parts to be ordered.

CHAPTER 8: TAKING CARE OF YOUR MACBOOK AIR M4

Cleaning and Maintaining Your MacBook Air M4

Your MacBook Air M4 is an investment, and just like any valuable item, taking care of it properly will ensure it lasts for years while maintaining its sleek, premium look. Regular cleaning and proper maintenance can also help keep it running smoothly and performing at its best. In this section, we'll cover practical, easy-to-follow tips to help you keep your MacBook Air M4 looking fresh and performing well.

Why Regular Cleaning is Important

Over time, dust, dirt, oil, and fingerprints naturally accumulate on your MacBook Air M4, especially on the screen, keyboard, and ports. Not only does this affect its appearance, but it can also impact performance. For example, dust in the ports can affect connectivity, while oil and grime on the keyboard can make typing uncomfortable and unsightly. Regular cleaning also reduces the chances of dust buildup inside your MacBook, which can lead to overheating and internal damage.

General Guidelines Before Cleaning

Before you start cleaning your MacBook, make sure you follow these important precautions:

1. **Turn off your MacBook**: It's always safest to turn off your MacBook Air M4 before cleaning. This reduces the risk of damaging any internal components or accidentally pressing keys while cleaning.

2. **Unplug all cables and accessories**: Remove any charging cables, USB devices, or other accessories that might be attached to your MacBook. This ensures that you avoid accidentally tugging on cables or damaging them.

3. **Use appropriate cleaning tools**: The materials you use for cleaning can have a big impact on how well you maintain your MacBook. Avoid using paper towels, household cleaners, or abrasive sponges, as they could scratch the surface.

Cleaning the Screen

Your MacBook Air M4's screen is one of its most important and delicate features, so it's essential to keep it clean without causing any damage.

What You'll Need:

- Microfiber cloth

- Distilled water (preferably) or a 70% isopropyl alcohol solution

- A soft-bristled brush (optional for corners)

Steps:

1. **Power off your MacBook**: Ensure the screen is turned off before cleaning.

2. **Dust the screen**: Use a dry microfiber cloth to gently wipe away dust from the screen. Start from the top and move down, avoiding any harsh pressure.

3. **Dampening the cloth**: If the screen has fingerprints or smudges, lightly dampen a microfiber cloth with distilled water or a 70% isopropyl alcohol solution. Never spray the solution directly onto the screen.

4. **Wiping the screen**: Gently wipe the screen with the dampened cloth in circular motions. Don't press too hard, as this could damage the screen or leave streaks.

5. **Dry the screen**: After cleaning, use a dry section of the microfiber cloth to buff the screen and remove any excess moisture or streaks.

Cleaning the Keyboard

The keyboard on your MacBook Air M4 can quickly accumulate dirt, oil, and crumbs, especially if you eat or drink near your laptop. A clean keyboard not only feels better to type on but can also prevent buildup from affecting performance.

What You'll Need:

- Soft-bristled brush or a can of compressed air

- Microfiber cloth

- 70% isopropyl alcohol (optional)

Steps:

1. **Turn off your MacBook**: Make sure the device is powered off to avoid accidentally pressing keys during the cleaning process.

2. **Dust the keyboard**: Use a soft-bristled brush or a can of compressed air to gently dislodge any dust, crumbs, or debris between the keys. Hold the MacBook at a slight angle to allow particles to fall out naturally.

3. **Wipe the keys**: Lightly dampen a microfiber cloth with 70% isopropyl alcohol or distilled water. Wipe the top surface of each key, being careful not to let any liquid seep between the keys.

4. **Dry the keyboard**: Use a dry microfiber cloth to remove any moisture and finish the cleaning process.

Tip: Avoid using excessive moisture, as liquid can seep under the keys and potentially damage the internal components.

Cleaning the Ports

Your MacBook Air M4's ports are where you connect essential devices like charging cables, external storage, and headphones. Dust or dirt buildup in these ports can impact performance and connectivity.

What You'll Need:

- A soft-bristled brush (small size works best)

- A can of compressed air

- Microfiber cloth

Steps:

1. **Power off your MacBook**: Always turn off the MacBook before cleaning the ports to avoid short-circuiting or causing any damage.

2. **Dust the ports**: Gently brush out any dust or debris from the USB-C, headphone jack, or any other ports. Use a soft-bristled brush to avoid scratching the inside of the ports.

3. **Use compressed air**: If there's stubborn dirt or dust, use short bursts of compressed air to blow it out. Hold the can at least 6 inches away from the ports to avoid damaging any internal components.

4. **Wipe down the exterior**: Use a dry microfiber cloth to wipe the exterior of the ports, removing any remaining dust or fingerprints.

Tip: Regularly clean the ports to avoid build-up that could interfere with charging or data transfer.

Cleaning the Bottom and Case

The bottom of your MacBook Air M4, especially if you often use it on different surfaces, can accumulate dust, oils, and even marks from where you set it down. Cleaning the case helps to maintain its pristine look.

What You'll Need:

- Microfiber cloth

- 70% isopropyl alcohol (optional)

- Soft-bristled brush

Steps:

1. **Turn off your MacBook**: For safety, always power off the MacBook before cleaning the exterior.

2. **Dust the bottom**: Use a soft-bristled brush to gently remove any dust or debris from the bottom of the MacBook, especially around the vents and feet.

3. **Wipe the exterior**: Dampen a microfiber cloth with a small amount of isopropyl alcohol or water. Wipe down the bottom of the MacBook, taking care to avoid getting moisture near the vents or ports.

4. **Dry the case**: Use a dry microfiber cloth to remove any moisture and buff the exterior of the case.

Cleaning the Touchpad

Your MacBook Air M4's touchpad is an essential input device, and keeping it clean will ensure smooth and responsive use. It's a high-touch area that can accumulate oils and smudges quickly.

What You'll Need:

- Microfiber cloth

- 70% isopropyl alcohol (optional)

Steps:

1. **Power off your MacBook**: As with the other parts, it's best to turn off the MacBook before cleaning.

2. **Wipe the touchpad**: Use a microfiber cloth dampened with a small amount of isopropyl alcohol or water to gently wipe the touchpad in circular motions.

3. **Dry the touchpad**: Buff the touchpad with a dry section of the microfiber cloth to ensure no moisture is left on the surface.

Maintaining the MacBook Air M4 for Longevity

Now that your MacBook is clean, let's go over some tips for long-term care and maintenance to keep it functioning at its best:

1. **Use a Case or Sleeve**: While the MacBook Air M4 is built to be durable, using a case or sleeve will help protect it from scratches and dents, especially when you're traveling or storing it.

2. **Keep It Cool**: Avoid using your MacBook on soft surfaces like beds or couches that can block the airflow and cause the system to overheat. Use it on hard, flat surfaces to help the cooling system work efficiently.

3. **Regular Software Updates**: Ensure your macOS is updated regularly to keep your system secure and optimized. Enabling automatic updates is a great way to ensure you're always up to date.

4. **Backup Your Data**: Regularly back up your important files using Time Machine or iCloud. This way, if anything happens to your MacBook, you won't lose your important documents and data.

Updating Software: How to Keep Your MacBook Secure and Up-to-Date

When you first power on your MacBook Air M4, it's exciting to dive right into everything it has to offer—whether it's the latest macOS version or all the shiny new features in the M4 chip. But just as important as the thrill of new technology is the ongoing need to keep your device updated. Software updates are the lifeblood of your MacBook's performance and security, and here's why you should never ignore them.

Why Software Updates Matter

You might wonder, "Why should I bother with updates every time I see a notification?" Well, here's the thing: macOS updates aren't just about adding new features or changing how things look. They are critical for a few major reasons:

- **Security Enhancements**: Hackers are always finding new ways to exploit vulnerabilities in software. With each update, Apple releases patches that fix known security issues, helping protect your personal data and privacy. Keeping your MacBook Air M4 up-to-date is one of the best defenses against malware, data breaches, and other cybersecurity threats.

- **Bug Fixes**: No software is perfect, and even macOS can have bugs. Updates fix these bugs to improve the overall stability and reliability of your system. Whether it's a glitch in the system, a slow-running app, or a feature that's just not behaving as it should, updates often address these issues.

- **Performance Improvements**: Along with security patches and bug fixes, updates often come with optimizations that can make your MacBook run smoother. Apple is constantly improving how macOS interacts with hardware, so with each update, your MacBook Air M4 may work more efficiently, consume less power, and feel faster overall.

- **New Features**: Software updates often come with exciting new features or improvements to existing ones. These could be anything from new macOS functionalities to fresh features for apps like Safari, Mail, or Photos. The M4 chip, for example, might see optimizations that improve its power and efficiency after each macOS update.

Enabling Automatic Updates

For those who want to ensure their MacBook Air M4 stays up-to-date without having to worry about it, macOS offers a very convenient feature: **automatic updates**. By enabling automatic updates, your MacBook Air M4 will download and install updates on its own, as long as it's connected to the internet. Here's how you can enable this feature:

1. **Click on the Apple Menu**: In the top-left corner of your screen, click on the Apple logo.

2. **Open System Preferences**: From the dropdown menu, select "System Preferences."

3. **Go to Software Update**: In the System Preferences window, click on the "Software Update" icon.

4. **Enable Automatic Updates**: In the Software Update section, you should see a checkbox that says "Automatically keep my Mac up to date." Make sure this box is checked. If it isn't, click it to enable automatic updates.

When you enable automatic updates, your MacBook will handle the update process for you, downloading the latest macOS updates in the background and installing them when it's convenient—usually when your MacBook isn't being used. This ensures your MacBook always stays up-to-date with the latest improvements, security patches, and bug fixes, with no manual intervention required.

But let's not stop there; you might want to customize how updates are handled.

Customizing Update Settings

macOS offers a few options to tailor how updates are installed. If you want a bit more control over when and how updates are downloaded or installed, follow these steps:

1. **Open System Preferences**: Go back to System Preferences, as mentioned earlier.

2. **Software Update Settings**: Within the Software Update section, click on the "Advanced" button (it's located on the bottom right).

3. **Choose Your Preferences**: In this section, you can choose which types of updates are automatically installed. You'll typically see options like:

   o **Check for updates**: Allows your MacBook to check for available updates automatically.

   o **Download new updates when available**: This will ensure the updates are downloaded automatically when they become available.

   o **Install macOS updates**: If enabled, this will install updates automatically without requiring your approval.

   o **Install app updates from the App Store**: This ensures any updates to apps you've downloaded from the App Store are installed automatically.

4. **Confirm Settings**: Once you've set your preferences, click **OK** to save them.

With these custom settings, you have the option to control when updates are installed, while still ensuring that important updates, such as macOS security patches, are not overlooked.

Manually Checking for Updates

Although enabling automatic updates ensures that your MacBook Air M4 is always up-to-date, there may be times when you want to check for updates yourself. Maybe you just heard about a new update release and want to install it right away, or perhaps you're experiencing issues and need the latest fixes. Here's how to manually check for software updates:

1. **Click on the Apple Menu**: Click the Apple logo in the top-left corner of your screen.

2. **Open System Preferences**: Select "System Preferences" from the dropdown menu.

3. **Go to Software Update**: Click on the "Software Update" option.

4. **Check for Updates**: Your MacBook will automatically check for any available updates. If there's an update available, you'll see an option to download and install it. If your system is up-to-date, it will tell you that no updates are available at the moment.

5. **Install the Update**: If an update is available, click "Update Now." The process might take a little time depending on the size of the update, and you may need to restart your MacBook once it's finished.

While your MacBook is downloading or installing an update, you can continue working, but be aware that certain updates might require a restart, so you may need to save your work before initiating the process.

Why Regular Updates Are Essential for Security

You've probably heard this a million times, but it bears repeating: **security is everything**. Keeping your MacBook Air M4 updated is the most straightforward way to safeguard your personal data and privacy. Here's how updates play a crucial role in keeping you secure:

- **Fixing Security Vulnerabilities**: Cybercriminals are always on the lookout for ways to exploit weaknesses in software, and once they discover these vulnerabilities, they're quick to act. Apple knows this, which is why it releases security updates to patch vulnerabilities as soon as they're discovered. By keeping your MacBook Air M4 up-to-date, you're making it much harder for cyber threats to target you.

- **Protection Against Malware**: Though macOS is generally more secure than many other operating systems, no system is invincible. Malware, adware, and phishing attacks still find their way onto Macs from time to time. Software updates often include specific patches to address these risks, making them an essential tool in defending against malware.

- **Ensuring Your Privacy**: Many macOS updates include privacy enhancements that ensure your data is being protected to the highest standards. Whether it's improving how data is encrypted or giving you more control over app permissions, software updates ensure that your MacBook Air M4 meets the latest privacy standards.

Staying Informed About Updates

Apple also provides **release notes** for every update. These release notes include details about what each update includes—whether it's security patches, new features, or bug fixes. To stay informed, visit Apple's official website or check the **System Preferences > Software Update** section where you can often find more information about each new version.

Wrapping It Up

Updating your MacBook Air M4 regularly is one of the simplest yet most important steps you can take to keep your device secure and running smoothly. With automatic updates, the process is nearly effortless. By ensuring your system is always up-to-date, you not only protect your data but also enjoy a better, more efficient performance.

So, whether you choose to let macOS handle the updates for you, or you like to check manually, just remember: keeping your MacBook Air M4 updated is key to unlocking its full potential. Don't let a single update pass you by— your MacBook will thank you for it!

Backing Up Your Data: Using Time Machine and iCloud

Backing up your data is one of the most important steps you can take to ensure the safety and security of your files. Whether it's precious family photos, important work documents, or personal files you can't afford to lose, having a reliable backup system is essential. Fortunately, with your MacBook Air M4, Apple offers two powerful and convenient options for backing up: **Time Machine** and **iCloud**. In this section, we'll walk you through how to use both options, highlight their advantages, and help you decide which one—or combination—is right for you.

What is Time Machine?

Time Machine is Apple's built-in backup feature, and it's an absolute game-changer. It's designed to work seamlessly with your MacBook to automatically back up your entire system, including your files, applications, settings, and system files. What makes Time Machine so useful is its ability to create incremental backups. This means that, over time, Time Machine only backs up the files that have changed since the last backup, making the process quick and efficient.

If anything ever goes wrong with your MacBook—whether it's a hardware failure, accidental file deletion, or even a system crash—Time Machine makes it incredibly easy to restore your data. You can either restore individual files or even perform a full system recovery, bringing everything back to how it was before the issue occurred.

How to Set Up Time Machine

Setting up Time Machine on your MacBook Air M4 is simple. Here's how to get started:

1. **Get an External Storage Device**:

   o Before you start backing up, you'll need an external hard drive, SSD, or a network-attached storage (NAS) device. Make sure the storage is large enough to hold all the data you want to back up. Apple recommends using a drive with at least twice the storage capacity of your Mac's hard drive for optimal backup space.

2. **Connect the External Drive**:

   o Plug your external storage device into one of the MacBook Air M4's USB or Thunderbolt ports. Your Mac should automatically detect the drive. If it's the first time connecting the device, you may be prompted to format it. Select "Use as Backup Disk" to set it up for Time Machine.

3. **Enable Time Machine**:

   o Go to the **Apple Menu** in the top-left corner of your screen and select **System Preferences**.

   o Click on **Time Machine**.

MACBOOK AIR M4 USER GUIDE

- In the Time Machine preferences window, click **Select Backup Disk** and choose your external storage device from the list.

- Once you've selected the drive, click **Use Disk**. You may be asked if you want to encrypt your backups; it's a good idea to do this for added security.

- Time Machine will now start backing up your Mac automatically every hour.

4. **Let Time Machine Do the Rest**:

- After the initial backup (which may take a while depending on how much data you have), Time Machine will continue to back up your data in the background. It will back up every hour, every day, and every week, keeping a full history of your files for the past month. You won't need to manually intervene—just let Time Machine run in the background and do its job.

Restoring Data with Time Machine

If you ever need to recover a file or restore your system, Time Machine makes it simple:

1. **Enter Time Machine**:

- Click the **Time Machine** icon in the menu bar (it looks like a clock with an arrow running in a circle) and select **Enter Time Machine**.

2. **Browse Your Backups**:

   o You'll see a timeline on the right side of the screen showing your backups. Use the arrows or the timeline to go back in time and find the specific backup you want to restore from. You can browse through your files just like you would in Finder.

3. **Restore Files**:

   o Once you've located the file or folder you want to recover, select it and click the **Restore** button. The file will be returned to its original location on your MacBook.

4. **Restore Your Entire System**:

   o If you need to restore your entire system—perhaps due to a major issue or system failure—restart your MacBook and hold down **Command + R** to enter **macOS Recovery**.

   o From there, you can choose the option to restore from a Time Machine backup and follow the on-screen instructions to restore your Mac to its previous state.

Advantages of Time Machine

- **Automatic Backups**: Once you set it up, Time Machine works in the background, backing up your Mac without requiring any manual effort. It keeps your files up to date with minimal intervention from you.

- **Granular Restoration**: You can restore individual files, entire folders, or your whole system. Time Machine gives you the flexibility to recover exactly what you need, whether it's one file or everything.

- **Incremental Backups**: Time Machine doesn't back up your entire system every time. Instead, it only backs up the changes made since the last backup, which makes it faster and more efficient.

- **Version History**: Time Machine stores multiple versions of your files. This means you can go back and retrieve older versions of documents, helping you avoid accidental data loss or mistakes.

What is iCloud?

While Time Machine is perfect for backing up data on an external device, iCloud is Apple's cloud-based storage solution, designed to seamlessly integrate with your MacBook Air M4. iCloud lets you store files, photos, documents, and more on Apple's secure cloud servers, making it easy to access your data from any Apple device, anywhere in the world.

One of iCloud's main benefits is that it automatically syncs your files across devices. This means you can save a document on your MacBook and instantly access it on your iPhone or iPad without needing to do anything extra. Plus, iCloud gives you 5GB of free storage, and you can purchase more if you need it.

How to Set Up iCloud Backup

1. **Sign Into iCloud**:

o First, make sure you're signed in with your Apple ID on your MacBook Air M4. Go to the **Apple Menu** and select **System Preferences**, then click **Apple ID**.

o Enter your Apple ID credentials and ensure that iCloud is activated.

2. **Choose What to Sync with iCloud**:

o In the **Apple ID** section of **System Preferences**, click **iCloud**.

o You'll see a list of services that can be synced with iCloud. These include **Photos**, **Documents**, **iCloud Drive**, **Mail**, **Calendars**, and more. Check the boxes next to the services you want to sync with iCloud.

3. **Using iCloud Drive**:

o iCloud Drive is where you can store and access all your documents. To access it, simply open **Finder** and click on **iCloud Drive** in the sidebar. You can drag and drop files into iCloud Drive for automatic syncing across your devices.

Restoring Data from iCloud

1. **Restore Files from iCloud Drive**:

o Open **Finder** and click on **iCloud Drive** in the sidebar.

o   Browse through your stored files, and if you need to restore any files, simply drag them from iCloud Drive back to your MacBook.

2. **Restore Photos and Videos from iCloud**:

   o   Open the **Photos** app on your MacBook.

   o   Any photos you've uploaded to iCloud will be available here. Simply select the photo or video you want to restore.

Advantages of iCloud

- **Seamless Integration Across Apple Devices**: iCloud syncs your data across all your Apple devices, so you can access it anytime, anywhere. No need for external drives or manual backups.

- **Easy File Sharing**: Share files with others directly from iCloud Drive, making collaboration or sharing photos, documents, and more simple and convenient.

- **Automatic Updates**: iCloud automatically backs up and syncs your data, ensuring that all your files are up to date across all devices. You don't have to worry about manually backing up files—it happens in the background.

- **Access from Anywhere**: iCloud allows you to access your files from any device with iCloud support, including Windows PCs via a browser, making it a versatile backup option.

Which Option Should You Choose: Time Machine or iCloud?

Both **Time Machine** and **iCloud** are excellent backup options, but they serve slightly different purposes. Here's how to decide which one to use—or whether you should use both:

- **Use Time Machine** if you want to back up your entire system, including your operating system, settings, and all your files. Time Machine is best for recovering from a complete system failure or restoring a large number of files at once.

- **Use iCloud** if you want seamless cloud storage for documents, photos, and files that you want to access across multiple devices. It's perfect for daily backups of files you regularly work with and want to have available everywhere.

For the best of both worlds, you can use **both**! Time Machine can back up your entire system to an external drive, while iCloud can keep your most important documents and photos securely in the cloud for easy access.

Protecting Your Privacy and Security with macOS

Your MacBook Air M4 is a powerful device that houses a wealth of personal information, from documents and photos to passwords and payment details.

It's crucial to set up your MacBook in a way that keeps your data safe and ensures your privacy is protected. In this section, we'll guide you through the essential security features that macOS offers, including setting up FileVault encryption, enabling firewall protection, and adjusting privacy settings for apps.

1. Enabling FileVault Encryption

One of the most important steps you can take to protect your MacBook Air M4 is to enable FileVault encryption. FileVault is a built-in macOS feature that encrypts your hard drive, making it nearly impossible for anyone to access your data without your password. This encryption is particularly useful if you ever lose your MacBook or it's stolen, as it ensures your personal information remains secure.

Here's how to enable FileVault:

1. Click on the **Apple Menu** (the apple logo at the top left of your screen).

2. Select **System Preferences**, then click on **Security & Privacy**.

3. Go to the **FileVault** tab.

4. Click the lock icon in the bottom-left corner to make changes, and enter your admin password.

5. Click **Turn On FileVault**.

FileVault will now start encrypting your drive in the background. This process may take some time, depending on the size of your data. Your

MacBook will notify you when encryption is complete. Once FileVault is active, your MacBook will ask for your password each time it boots up, making it more secure.

Why FileVault is Important:

- **Prevents unauthorized access**: Even if someone gets their hands on your MacBook, they won't be able to access your files without the decryption password.

- **Full disk encryption**: FileVault encrypts everything on your drive, including documents, applications, and even system files, ensuring all your data stays protected.

2. Setting Up Firewall Protection

A firewall is your first line of defense against malicious activity trying to gain unauthorized access to your MacBook's network. macOS includes a built-in firewall that can be easily turned on to block unwanted connections and enhance your privacy.

To enable the firewall on your MacBook:

1. Open **System Preferences** and click on **Security & Privacy**.

2. Select the **Firewall** tab.

3. Click the lock icon to make changes and enter your admin password.

4. Click **Turn On Firewall**.

Once the firewall is active, your MacBook will monitor incoming and outgoing network traffic. It will block any unwanted connections from apps or services that are trying to access your device without your permission.

Additional Firewall Settings:

- **Firewall Options**: If you want to further customize your firewall settings, click **Firewall Options**. Here, you can allow or block specific apps from accepting incoming connections. For example, if you're using a secure app like a VPN, you can allow it through the firewall, while blocking others.

- **Stealth Mode**: Enable this option to make your MacBook "invisible" on the network. This means your device won't respond to unsolicited network requests, making it harder for hackers to identify it.

The firewall in macOS is already highly effective for most users, but enabling it adds an extra layer of protection, especially when you're connected to public Wi-Fi networks.

3. Using Privacy Settings for Apps

macOS gives you full control over which apps can access your personal information, such as your location, contacts, microphone, and camera. By adjusting these privacy settings, you can ensure that only the apps you trust have access to sensitive data.

Here's how to adjust privacy settings on your MacBook:

1. Open **System Preferences** and click on **Security & Privacy**.

MACBOOK AIR M4 USER GUIDE

2. Select the **Privacy** tab. Here, you'll see a list of categories that control which apps have access to specific types of data.

3. To make changes, click the lock icon at the bottom-left corner and enter your admin password.

You'll now be able to see a list of apps and their permissions. Let's go over some of the most important categories you should review:

- **Location Services**: This allows apps to access your geographic location. Review which apps have access to your location and disable any apps that don't need it. For example, map or weather apps typically need this, but games or social media apps might not.

- **Contacts**: This section controls which apps can access your contact list. If an app requests access to your contacts but you don't want it, simply uncheck the box next to that app.

- **Camera & Microphone**: macOS allows you to control which apps can use your camera and microphone. For your privacy, make sure only apps you trust have permission to access these devices, such as FaceTime or Skype for video calls.

- **Analytics & Improvements**: You can choose to share or limit data about how you use your MacBook for improving Apple's services. Disable this if you prefer not to share analytics data.

Why Privacy Settings Matter:

- **Protects your personal information**: By controlling app permissions, you prevent apps from accessing sensitive data like your location or private conversations.

- **Prevents misuse**: Some apps may use your data in ways you don't expect, such as tracking your location or recording audio without your knowledge. Adjusting privacy settings prevents this from happening.

4. Enabling Two-Factor Authentication

For added security, consider enabling **Two-Factor Authentication (2FA)** for your Apple ID. This feature provides an extra layer of protection by requiring you to verify your identity through a second device or code when logging into your Apple ID account. This way, even if someone gains access to your password, they won't be able to access your Apple account without your second authentication factor.

Here's how to enable Two-Factor Authentication:

1. Open **System Preferences** and click on **Apple ID**.

2. In the **Password & Security** section, click **Turn On Two-Factor Authentication**.

3. Follow the on-screen instructions to set it up.

Enabling 2FA will give you peace of mind, knowing that your Apple ID and all connected services are secure.

CHAPTER 9: TIPS AND TRICKS FOR EVERYDAY USE

Must-Know Keyboard Shortcuts to Work Smarter

As a MacBook Air M4 user, mastering keyboard shortcuts will significantly speed up your daily tasks and improve your overall workflow. Apple's macOS is designed with efficiency in mind, and learning just a few essential shortcuts will make your experience much smoother. Whether you're a beginner or a seasoned Mac user, this section will provide you with the keyboard shortcuts that will help you navigate macOS, manage apps, and perform basic tasks more effectively.

Let's dive into the shortcuts that you absolutely need to know!

1. Navigating macOS

The MacBook Air M4's macOS offers many intuitive ways to navigate around your computer, and using keyboard shortcuts can help you breeze through tasks that would otherwise take longer with a mouse. Here are the shortcuts you should be using to move around your MacBook like a pro:

Command (⌘) + Space

- **What it does:** Opens Spotlight search.

- **Why it's useful:** You can search for anything on your MacBook— apps, files, folders, web searches, and more—without clicking around. Just hit this shortcut, type what you're looking for, and hit Enter. Fast, simple, and a game-changer for efficiency!

Command (⌘) + Tab

- **What it does:** Switch between open apps.

- **Why it's useful:** Rather than clicking through the Dock or minimizing windows, just hold down Command and tap Tab to quickly cycle through your open applications. This saves you time when you need to jump from one app to another without losing focus.

Command (⌘) + ` (backtick)

- **What it does:** Switch between windows of the same app.

- **Why it's useful:** When you have multiple windows open in the same app (say, multiple Safari windows), this shortcut allows you to toggle between them with ease. No need to minimize or find the correct window!

Control + Tab

- **What it does:** Switch between tabs in the same app (works in apps like Safari, Finder, etc.).

- **Why it's useful:** If you have several tabs open within an app, this shortcut lets you cycle through them without clicking. It's like flipping through pages of a book in a flash.

2. Managing Apps

Once you've learned how to navigate macOS, managing multiple apps and windows becomes a whole lot easier. These shortcuts will help you manage your workspace efficiently:

Command (⌘) + H

- **What it does:** Hide the current app.

- **Why it's useful:** If you're working on something and need to quickly clear up your workspace without closing everything, Command + H will hide the app you're currently using. You can access it again from the Dock or by using Command + Tab to cycle back.

Command (⌘) + Q

- **What it does:** Quit the current app.

- **Why it's useful:** This shortcut is a fast way to close any app entirely. If you're finished with an app and don't need it running in the background, use Command + Q to quit it. It's much faster than clicking on the app's exit button.

Command (⌘) + M

- **What it does:** Minimize the current window.

- **Why it's useful:** When you're multitasking, minimizing windows can help declutter your workspace. Rather than clicking the minimize button, use Command + M to quickly send a window to the Dock without closing it.

Command (⌘) + W

- **What it does:** Close the current window.

- **Why it's useful:** This shortcut will close the current window without quitting the app. It's especially helpful when you want to get rid of a cluttered window but keep the app open for later use.

Command (⌘) + Option + Escape

- **What it does:** Force quit apps.

- **Why it's useful:** If an app becomes unresponsive and you can't close it the normal way, this shortcut will open the Force Quit menu. From there, you can select the app you want to quit. It's a lifesaver when things freeze up!

3. Performing Basic Tasks

Now that you've learned how to navigate macOS and manage your apps, let's dive into some essential shortcuts for handling basic tasks quickly and efficiently.

Command (⌘) + C / Command (⌘) + V

- **What it does:** Copy and paste, respectively.

- **Why it's useful:** These classic shortcuts allow you to copy any selected text, files, or images and paste them wherever you need them. It's one of the most essential shortcuts for getting things done quickly.

Command (⌘) + X

- **What it does:** Cut the selected text or file.

- **Why it's useful:** If you need to move something rather than just copy it, Command + X will cut the selected text or file so that you can paste it elsewhere. It's great for organizing your files and folders quickly.

Command (⌘) + Z

- **What it does:** Undo the last action.

- **Why it's useful:** Made a mistake? Just press Command + Z to undo your last action. This works in almost every app, from text editing to file management, and is essential for fixing errors in a pinch.

Command (⌘) + Shift + Z

- **What it does:** Redo the last undone action.

- **Why it's useful:** After undoing an action, if you want to redo it, Command + Shift + Z lets you bring it back with ease. It's like the opposite of Command + Z, but equally powerful.

Command (⌘) + A

- **What it does:** Select all items in a window or document.

- **Why it's useful:** When you need to select everything—whether it's text in a document or all the files in a folder—Command + A makes it quick and easy. After selecting everything, you can copy, cut, or delete in one go.

Command (⌘) + Shift + 3 / Command (⌘) + Shift + 4

- **What it does:** Take a screenshot (entire screen or selection).

- **Why it's useful:** If you need to capture something on your screen, these shortcuts are a must. Command + Shift + 3 takes a screenshot of the entire screen, while Command + Shift + 4 lets you select a portion of the screen. You can use this to capture quick visuals for work, notes, or sharing.

Command (⌘) + F

- **What it does:** Open the Find bar in an app or document.

- **Why it's useful:** If you need to find specific text or items within a document, web page, or folder, Command + F opens a search box to help you quickly locate it. This is incredibly helpful when you're dealing with large amounts of information.

4. File Management

Organizing files and folders efficiently is key to working smart on your MacBook Air M4. These shortcuts will save you a lot of time when managing your documents and projects.

Command (⌘) + N

- **What it does:** Open a new Finder window or document.
- **Why it's useful:** This shortcut opens a new window for browsing your files or creating a new document in any app that supports it. It's essential when you need to keep several documents open or work with multiple Finder windows.

Command (⌘) + Shift + N

- **What it does:** Create a new folder in Finder.
- **Why it's useful:** When organizing files, creating a new folder can be a tedious task if you don't know the shortcut. Command + Shift + N immediately creates a new folder, so you can organize your files without interrupting your workflow.

Command (⌘) + Delete

- **What it does:** Move selected items to the Trash.
- **Why it's useful:** When you need to delete files, Command + Delete quickly moves the selected items to the Trash without the need to drag them. It's much faster than using the mouse!

5. System Shortcuts

Sometimes you need quick access to system settings or perform tasks like shutting down your MacBook Air M4. Here are the shortcuts that'll help you manage your system more effectively.

Control + Command (⌘) + Q

- **What it does:** Lock your MacBook.

- **Why it's useful:** If you need to step away from your MacBook and want to lock it quickly, just press Control + Command + Q. This locks your screen and prevents others from accessing your data until you enter your password.

Command (⌘) + Option + Power Button

- **What it does:** Put your MacBook to sleep.

- **Why it's useful:** Quickly put your MacBook to sleep when you're not using it to save energy. This shortcut is helpful when you're on the go and don't want to close all your apps.

Command (⌘) + Option + Escape

- **What it does:** Open the Force Quit menu.

- **Why it's useful:** If an app is unresponsive and you can't close it, use this shortcut to open the Force Quit menu. From there, you can select the app and force it to quit, saving you from any frustration when things freeze up.

The Best Touchpad Gestures for a Seamless Experience

The MacBook Air M4's touchpad is not just a simple pointing device—it's a powerful tool that allows you to interact with macOS in a way that's intuitive, fluid, and fast. With a few simple gestures, you can navigate, zoom, and multitask seamlessly, improving your overall productivity and experience. Whether you're a beginner or a seasoned Mac user, mastering these gestures will make using your MacBook Air feel more natural, fluid, and efficient.

In this section, we'll explore the best touchpad gestures that every MacBook Air M4 user should know. We'll break them down into basic gestures to get you started and then move into some advanced tricks to enhance your workflow.

Basic Touchpad Gestures: Mastering the Fundamentals

1. Single Tap to Click

This one's the simplest of them all. Just tap once on the touchpad to click—just like pressing a mouse button. This gesture is so natural that it becomes second nature very quickly. It's perfect for selecting items, opening applications, or confirming your choice.

2. Double Tap to Open or Select

Double-tapping is another essential gesture that you'll use frequently. It's the go-to gesture for opening files, folders, or apps. When you're navigating through Finder or your desktop, simply double-tap an icon to open it. This gesture works just like double-clicking with a mouse, making it a crucial part of your MacBook experience.

3. Right-Click with Two Fingers

Unlike some traditional laptops where the right-click option is hidden or confusing, on the MacBook Air M4, all you need to do is tap the touchpad with **two fingers**. This opens up a context menu, giving you additional options like copy, paste, or delete. This is a key feature that helps you quickly access shortcuts and additional functions without needing to navigate through menus.

4. Scrolling with Two Fingers

The two-finger scroll is a must-know gesture for web browsing, reading, or navigating through long documents. Just place two fingers on the touchpad and slide them up or down to scroll. Whether you're scrolling through a webpage or a document, this gesture is natural and seamless.

Zooming In and Out with Pinch-to-Zoom

5. Pinch-to-Zoom

One of the most satisfying gestures on the MacBook Air M4 is **pinch-to-zoom**. Whether you're zooming in on a picture, a map, or a webpage, all you need to do is place two fingers on the touchpad and either spread them apart (zoom in) or pinch them together (zoom out). This gesture is perfect for adjusting the view of images, text, or websites, and it's especially helpful when you want to get a closer look at a detail without fiddling with keyboard shortcuts or menus.

Advanced Touchpad Gestures: Taking Your Productivity to the Next Level

6. Swiping Between Full-Screen Apps

If you're someone who juggles multiple apps and windows on a regular basis, you'll love the **swipe between full-screen apps** gesture. Simply swipe **three fingers left or right** on the touchpad to quickly switch between full-screen apps. This is ideal when you're working across different apps, like a web browser, word processor, or design tool, and you need to jump between them quickly without losing focus.

7. Mission Control with Three-Finger Swipe Up

Mission Control is an essential feature on macOS that lets you view all your open windows at once, making multitasking a breeze. To activate it, simply swipe **three fingers upward** on the touchpad. This will give you a bird's-eye view of all your active windows, apps, and desktops. It's a fantastic way to find an open window or quickly switch between tasks. Once you've activated Mission Control, you can click on any window to bring it to the foreground, making your workflow more efficient.

8. App Exposé with Three-Finger Swipe Down

Want to quickly see all open windows for a specific app? Try **swiping three fingers downward** on the touchpad. This gesture activates App Exposé, which shows all the windows of the app you're currently using. This is incredibly useful if you have multiple documents or browser tabs open in the same app and want to switch between them quickly.

9. Show Desktop with a Four-Finger Spread

Sometimes, you just need to clear your workspace to get a better view. To show the desktop, simply **spread four fingers apart** on the touchpad. This gesture minimizes all open windows and lets you see your desktop. It's a handy way to declutter your screen when you need to focus on a file or open a new app. Once you're ready, just pinch your fingers back together to restore your windows to their previous position.

Extra Touchpad Tricks to Enhance Your Experience

10. Dragging Items with Three Fingers

If you're organizing files or moving windows around on your desktop, the **three-finger drag** can make the process a lot smoother. To use this gesture, go to your **System Preferences** and enable "Three Finger Drag" under the "Trackpad" settings. Once activated, you can click and hold with three fingers to drag items around on your screen. This makes rearranging windows and organizing files quick and intuitive.

11. Showing Notification Center

Want to quickly access your notifications? Simply swipe **two fingers from right to left** on the touchpad. This gesture opens the Notification Center, where you can view recent notifications, calendar events, and quick access to widgets. It's perfect for staying on top of your messages, updates, and tasks without interrupting your workflow.

12. Zooming in Apps (Using Safari, Maps, Photos, etc.)

Pinch-to-zoom isn't just for images and web pages. You can also zoom in on things like maps and photos. In Safari, for example, pinch to zoom in on web pages for a closer look at text or images. In Photos, you can zoom in on pictures for a better view of the details. This gesture works across many apps, making it a versatile tool for both work and play.

Pro Tip: Customize Your Touchpad Settings

Did you know that you can adjust how your touchpad behaves? Go to **System Preferences** > **Trackpad**, and you'll find options to customize your gestures. You can adjust the tracking speed, enable or disable specific gestures, or even turn off the tap-to-click function if you prefer clicking in a more traditional way. This level of customization allows you to tailor your MacBook Air M4 experience to your personal preferences.

Using Preview, Photos, and Notes to Stay Organized

In today's fast-paced digital world, keeping everything organized can often feel like a task of Herculean proportions. Whether you're juggling work documents, personal photos, or your daily thoughts, the key to staying on top of things is using the right tools. Fortunately, with your MacBook Air M4, you have access to three powerful apps—Preview, Photos, and Notes—that can make organizing documents, images, and personal notes a breeze.

Let's dive into how these apps can help you manage your digital life more efficiently.

Preview: Your Digital File Organizer

When it comes to handling documents, images, or PDFs, Preview is a game-changer. While it's often overlooked as a simple viewer, Preview is far more capable than most people realize. Here's how you can use it to streamline your workflow:

1. Organizing and Editing PDFs

If you work with PDFs regularly, Preview is your best friend. Not only can it open almost any PDF file, but it also lets you perform basic edits, which saves you from having to rely on third-party software. Here's how to make the most of it:

- **Mark Up PDFs**: Preview allows you to highlight text, add notes, or even draw directly on a PDF. This is useful for annotating documents or reviewing contracts before sending them out.

- **Combine Multiple PDFs**: If you need to merge several PDFs into one document, Preview makes it simple. Just open all the files you want to combine, then drag and drop them into the Preview sidebar to merge them into one seamless document.

- **Rearranging Pages**: Need to reorder the pages in a PDF? Simply click and drag the pages in the sidebar to rearrange them to your liking. This feature is incredibly useful when you're working with scanned documents or reports.

- **Convert Files**: Preview also lets you export PDFs as images (JPEG, PNG) or other formats like TIFF. This makes it easy to convert a document into a format that suits your needs, whether you're sharing a picture or working with a different software.

2. Viewing and Managing Images

Preview is not just for documents; it's a fantastic tool for managing images as well. Whether you're dealing with high-resolution photos or simple screenshots, Preview allows you to quickly view and make simple edits to your images.

- **Quick Preview**: If you're browsing through multiple images, Preview makes it simple to quickly glance at any image file by simply double-clicking on it. You don't have to worry about opening multiple apps, as Preview will handle most common image formats like JPEG, PNG, and TIFF.

- **Cropping and Adjusting**: Need to crop an image or make some quick adjustments? Preview allows you to crop, rotate, and adjust the color balance of your images. It also provides basic tools like adjusting brightness, contrast, and exposure—perfect for quick edits without the need for a more complex program.

- **Image Annotation**: If you need to make notes on your images— perhaps circling an area or adding arrows—Preview has simple annotation tools that let you do just that. This is great for those times when you want to highlight something specific on an image for later review.

Photos: Keeping Your Memories and Pictures Neatly Organized

The Photos app on your MacBook Air M4 isn't just for storing photos; it's a robust tool for organizing and managing your entire photo collection. Whether you're a casual user or a photography enthusiast, Photos has everything you need to keep your pictures in order. Here's how to get the most out of it:

1. Organizing Albums and Folders

One of the best features of the Photos app is the ability to organize your photos into albums and folders, which helps keep everything neatly arranged.

- **Creating Albums**: You can create albums based on events, vacations, or any other theme you like. For example, you might create an album for family gatherings, travel photos, or just a collection of your favorite shots. Creating albums helps keep your photos grouped by subject matter, making it much easier to find specific images later.

- **Using Smart Albums**: If you want Photos to automatically organize your images for you, try using Smart Albums. These albums are based on specific criteria such as date, location, or even keywords. For example, you can create a Smart Album that collects all photos taken in a certain location or during a specific time period.

- **Tagging and Search**: Tags make it easy to search for photos. If you add tags to your photos, such as "vacation," "birthday," or "work," you can quickly find specific images by searching with those keywords.

2. Enhancing Your Photos

Photos isn't just an organization tool—it's also great for editing and improving your pictures. With built-in editing tools, you can enhance your photos without needing to open a complex editing app.

- **Basic Editing**: Photos provides essential editing tools like cropping, rotating, and adjusting the exposure, contrast, and saturation of your photos. If you've taken a photo that doesn't quite look right, Photos makes it easy to fix it.

- **Filters and Effects**: Photos also comes with a variety of filters and effects that can help add some style to your pictures. Whether you want to make your photo look vintage or add a vibrant pop of color, there's a filter for it.

- **Auto-Enhance**: If you're in a rush and don't want to fuss with manual adjustments, Photos has an auto-enhance feature that analyzes your image and applies the best adjustments for better quality. This is perfect for users who just want to improve their photos quickly with minimal effort.

3. Sharing Your Photos

Once you've organized and enhanced your photos, Photos makes it incredibly easy to share them with friends and family. You can quickly send photos via email, share them on social media, or use AirDrop to send them to other Apple devices. This makes Photos not just a storage solution but also a powerful sharing tool.

Notes: The Ultimate Tool for Keeping Track of Everything

If you're someone who's always jotting down ideas, keeping track of tasks, or just writing personal thoughts, the Notes app on your MacBook Air M4 is your digital notebook. It's simple, fast, and incredibly flexible. Here's how to use it effectively for organization:

1. Creating and Organizing Notes

With Notes, it's easy to create a new note and start typing right away. The interface is clean and minimalist, so you're not distracted by unnecessary features. Here's how to keep your notes organized:

- **Folders**: Just like with Photos, you can organize your notes into folders. For example, you might have folders for personal notes, work-related tasks, shopping lists, or even project ideas. Using folders helps you keep your notes neatly categorized.

- **Pinning Important Notes**: If you have a note that you reference frequently, you can pin it to the top of your Notes app. This makes sure that it's always easy to access without having to search for it.

- **Checklists and To-Dos**: Notes also allows you to create checklists. If you're planning a project or making a shopping list, you can check off items as you complete them. This helps you stay on top of your tasks without having to switch to a separate to-do app.

2. Collaborating with Others

Notes isn't just for personal use; it's great for collaboration too. You can share notes with others and make live edits together. This is particularly useful for team projects or planning events with friends.

- **Sharing Notes**: You can share notes with others via iCloud. Once shared, collaborators can view and edit the note in real-time. Whether you're planning a trip, working on a group project, or sharing a list with a family member, Notes makes collaboration easy.

3. Adding Multimedia to Notes

Notes also allows you to add multimedia content, making it a more versatile tool for organization.

- **Inserting Photos and Documents**: You can drag and drop images, PDFs, and other documents directly into your notes. This is great for keeping all related information in one place. For example, you could attach a receipt image to your shopping list note, or include an article snippet in your work-related notes.

- **Sketching in Notes**: If you need to draw or make a quick sketch, Notes includes a built-in drawing tool that lets you create doodles, diagrams, or handwritten notes right inside the app.

Tips for Using Safari, Mail, and Calendar Efficiently

In today's fast-paced world, staying organized and efficient can make a huge difference in your daily productivity. Fortunately, the MacBook Air M4, with its powerful M4 chip and seamless integration of macOS, offers excellent tools to streamline your workflow. Safari, Mail, and Calendar are three of the most-used apps on your MacBook, and when used correctly, they can save you time and keep you on top of things.

Let's dive into actionable tips for getting the most out of Safari, Mail, and Calendar, tailored to make your life a little easier.

Safari: Mastering the Web

Safari is more than just a browser; it's a tool that, when optimized, can boost your productivity. Here are some ways to make Safari work harder for you:

1. Manage Tabs Efficiently

You've probably experienced the frustration of having too many tabs open at once. It's easy to get overwhelmed and lose track of what's important. Here's how to keep tabs organized:

- **Use Tab Groups**: macOS allows you to organize your tabs into groups. You can create tab groups for different tasks, such as "Work," "Research," or "Shopping." To create a new tab group, click on the "Sidebar" button in Safari, then click "New Tab Group" from the options. This will help you stay organized and reduce clutter.

- **Pin Tabs**: If there are websites you frequently visit, such as your email or a project management tool, pin those tabs. To do this, right-click on a tab and select "Pin Tab." Pinned tabs are smaller and always open, making them easily accessible and saving you the hassle of searching for them every time you open Safari.

- **Use the "Tab Overview" Feature**: For quick navigation, use the "Tab Overview" feature, which shows all your tabs in a grid format. You can quickly scroll through and find the tab you need. To access it, click the tab icon on the top right corner of your Safari window.

2. Customize Safari Settings for Privacy and Speed

Privacy and speed are two major concerns when browsing the internet. Here's how to adjust Safari settings for optimal use:

- **Enable Privacy Features**: Safari on macOS offers robust privacy protections. Under **Safari > Preferences > Privacy**, enable features like "Prevent Cross-Site Tracking" and "Block All Cookies." This will ensure that websites can't track your browsing behavior across the web, helping you stay private and secure.

- **Block Pop-ups and Ads**: Annoying pop-ups and intrusive ads can slow down your browsing experience. Go to **Safari > Preferences > Websites** and set the pop-up blocker to "Block and Notify" or "Block." You can also install ad-blocking extensions, which will reduce distractions and improve page load times.

- **Use iCloud Sync**: If you use Safari on multiple devices, iCloud Sync is a game-changer. Ensure Safari is set to sync across all your Apple devices so you can pick up right where you left off, whether you're on your MacBook, iPhone, or iPad.

3. Take Advantage of Reader Mode

If you're reading an article or blog, enable Safari's Reader Mode to strip away all the unnecessary ads and distractions. To activate it, click on the Reader icon in the URL bar (it looks like a series of lines). This will provide a clean, easy-to-read format, making reading more enjoyable.

Mail: Streamlining Your Email Management

Your email inbox can quickly become overwhelming with spam, work emails, and personal messages. But don't worry! Here are some tips to keep your Mail app organized and efficient:

1. Set Up Folders and Rules

To keep your inbox tidy, create folders to categorize your emails. You can create a folder for work, another for personal emails, and even one for newsletters or subscriptions. To create a folder:

- In the Mail app, go to **Mailbox > New Mailbox**, and then name it according to the type of emails it will contain (e.g., "Work," "Personal," "Newsletters").

Next, use **Rules** to automatically sort incoming emails into these folders. Go to **Mail > Preferences > Rules**, and click **Add Rule**. For example, you can set up a rule to move all emails from your boss directly to the "Work" folder. This way, you don't need to manually sort emails.

2. Use VIPs to Prioritize Important Emails

The VIP feature in Mail allows you to flag important contacts and receive notifications when you get emails from them. This can help you focus on high-priority messages and avoid missing anything urgent.

- To mark someone as a VIP, open an email from that person, right-click on their name in the email header, and select **Add to VIPs**. Once they're added, their emails will stand out in your inbox, and you'll receive a notification whenever they send a new message.

3. Search Smarter

Searching for old emails can be a pain, especially if your inbox is cluttered. To search more effectively:

- Use **Mail's Search Bar** and type specific keywords, email addresses, or subjects. The search results will be filtered by relevant messages. You can also narrow down results by clicking on the categories like "Attachments" or "From."

- Additionally, you can use **Search Suggestions** to search by specific criteria, like date ranges or flagged emails.

4. Set Up Signatures

If you send a lot of emails, having a professional signature can save time. You can create multiple signatures for different purposes (work, personal, etc.).

- Go to **Mail > Preferences > Signatures**, and click the "+" button to create a new signature. You can also specify which signature to use for new emails and replies, so you don't have to manually add them each time.

Calendar: Mastering Your Schedule

The Calendar app on your MacBook Air M4 is an invaluable tool for managing your time. Here are some tips to keep your schedule organized and stay on top of important dates:

1. Create Multiple Calendars for Different Aspects of Your Life

Using different calendars for work, personal events, and even family activities can help you stay organized without mixing up events. You can view all your calendars at once or focus on just one to stay organized.

- To create a new calendar, go to **File > New Calendar** in the Calendar app. Choose a color for each calendar, so it's easy to distinguish them.

2. Set Reminders for Important Events

Don't rely on memory alone—set reminders to notify you before important events. You can set a reminder to alert you minutes, hours, or days before an event. You can also set multiple reminders, like a "10 minutes before" and "1 day before" alert.

- To set a reminder, click on an event, click "Edit," and under **Alert**, choose when you'd like to receive a reminder. You can select options like "Message with sound" or even have it email you a notification.

3. Use Siri to Add Events and Set Reminders

With Siri, you don't even need to type anything to add a new event. Just say, "Hey Siri, schedule a meeting for 3 PM tomorrow," and Siri will add it directly to your Calendar.

MACBOOK AIR M4 USER GUIDE

4. Sync Your Calendar with iCloud and Other Devices

Sync your Calendar with iCloud to ensure that your events are accessible from all your Apple devices. If you use other calendar services, such as Google Calendar, you can add those to your Calendar app as well.

- To sync, go to **System Preferences > Apple ID > iCloud**, and make sure **Calendars** is checked. You'll now have access to your calendar on all your Apple devices.

5. Set Up Time Zones for Events

If you travel frequently or work with people in different time zones, it's crucial to keep track of the correct time zone for your events. You can set the time zone for individual events to ensure you don't miss anything due to time zone differences.

- To set the time zone, open an event in Calendar, click **Edit**, and then under **Time Zone**, select the correct one.

CHAPTER 10: GETTING THE MOST OUT OF MACOS

Hidden Features You Should Know About

macOS is known for its sleek design, smooth performance, and user-friendly experience. But beyond its surface-level simplicity, macOS has some hidden features that can really elevate your productivity, organization, and overall workflow. These lesser-known gems can make a huge difference for users who want to work smarter and faster. In this section, we'll uncover a few of these hidden features that you might not have discovered yet.

Let's dive into how you can make the most of **Quick Look**, **Finder Tabs**, and **Stacks**—all features that can streamline your workflow and add efficiency to your day.

Quick Look: Preview Files Instantly

How many times have you needed to quickly check a document or image but didn't want to open it fully? That's where **Quick Look** comes in. This feature allows you to preview almost any file with just a quick press of the spacebar—no need to open it in a specific app. It's a simple but powerful tool that can save you tons of time.

How It Works:

1. **Preview a File**: Select any file on your MacBook, whether it's a PDF, image, video, or text document.

2. **Press the Spacebar**: With the file selected, just press the spacebar on your keyboard. A preview of the file will pop up, showing you its contents.

3. **Navigate Through Files**: You can use the left and right arrow keys to flip through multiple files in a folder without needing to open them one by one.

4. **Quick Actions**: For PDFs, you can even highlight text, rotate images, or make annotations—straight from the Quick Look preview.

Why It's Useful:

Quick Look is fantastic for those moments when you don't need to fully open a file but just need a glimpse. Need to check the contents of a document? Quick Look's got you. Want to make sure the right image is selected for a project? Just hit space, and you're good to go. This small feature saves you a lot of clicking and jumping between apps, making your process much smoother.

Finder Tabs: Organize Your Files Like a Pro

If you've ever used multiple windows in Finder, you know how messy it can get. Juggling several windows and trying to find the right one can feel like a game of hide and seek. But **Finder Tabs** offer a cleaner, more organized way to manage multiple files, similar to how tabs work in web browsers like Safari.

How It Works:

1. **Open Finder**: First, open a Finder window as you normally would.

2. **Create Tabs**: To create a new tab, press **Command + T** or select "New Tab" from the "File" menu in Finder.

3. **Navigate Between Tabs**: You can easily switch between different tabs by clicking on them, or use **Command + Shift +]** to move right and **Command + Shift + [** to move left.

4. **Drag and Drop Files**: You can drag files from one tab to another, making it incredibly easy to organize and move files between folders.

Why It's Useful:

Finder Tabs are an absolute game-changer when it comes to file management. Instead of opening several Finder windows and cluttering your screen, you can keep everything in one window, neatly organized in different tabs. Whether you're working on a research project with multiple folders open or juggling several documents for a report, you can keep all your files in one place and switch between them with ease. Plus, it makes navigating your MacBook more intuitive and less overwhelming.

Stacks: Keep Your Desktop Neat and Tidy

If you're like many MacBook users, your desktop might become a dumping ground for files. You might find yourself constantly minimizing windows to

MACBOOK AIR M4 USER GUIDE

find that one file you need—sound familiar? Enter **Stacks**—a feature designed to organize your desktop and keep everything in neat, sorted piles.

How It Works:

1. **Enable Stacks**: Right-click anywhere on your desktop and select "Use Stacks." This automatically organizes all your files into groups by type, such as Documents, PDFs, Images, and more.

2. **Customizing Stacks**: You can adjust how your files are organized. Click **View** in the menu bar, and then choose your preferred grouping method—by kind, date, or tags.

3. **Expanding a Stack**: To view the files inside a stack, just click on the stack, and it will expand to show the files within it.

4. **Dragging Files into Stacks**: You can easily drag files into the appropriate stack, making it simple to stay organized as you work.

Why It's Useful:

Stacks are perfect for anyone who struggles with a cluttered desktop. By automatically organizing your files, they eliminate visual chaos, so you can focus on your work rather than hunting for files. You don't have to worry about accidentally dropping files in the wrong place, and you can keep your desktop neat without losing access to anything. Whether you're working on a big project or just need a way to manage all the files piling up, Stacks will help you stay on top of things.

Bonus Hidden Gems: A Few More Features You'll Love

While Quick Look, Finder Tabs, and Stacks are some of the more powerful features to help streamline your workflow, macOS has many other small features that can make your life easier:

Spotlight Search

Quickly find anything on your Mac—files, apps, and even web search results. Just hit **Command + Space**, type in what you're looking for, and let Spotlight do the heavy lifting. It's your personal assistant for everything on your MacBook.

Hot Corners

Assign actions to each corner of your screen—such as launching Mission Control, showing the desktop, or starting a screen saver—by simply moving your mouse to that corner. This is a quick and efficient way to access different features.

Preview File Markup

In the Preview app, you can not only view PDFs and images but also annotate them with shapes, text, and even signatures. This is perfect for reviewing documents or adding comments to a presentation.

Keyboard Shortcuts

macOS is full of keyboard shortcuts that can help speed up your workflow. For example, pressing **Command + Option + Esc** opens the Force Quit menu, and **Command + Tab** lets you quickly switch between open apps.

Syncing and Sharing with Other Devices

One of the most powerful features of the MacBook Air M4 is its seamless integration with the Apple ecosystem. Whether you're using an iPhone, iPad, Apple Watch, or any other Apple device, syncing and sharing content between these devices has never been easier. With a few simple settings, you can ensure that your photos, contacts, files, and even clipboard data are automatically synced and easily shared across all your Apple devices.

This chapter will guide you through how to sync and share content between your MacBook Air M4 and other Apple devices, using iCloud, AirDrop, and Universal Clipboard. By the end of this section, you'll be able to move effortlessly between your devices, making sure that your important content is always accessible wherever you go.

1. iCloud: Syncing Your Data Across Devices

iCloud is Apple's cloud storage service that allows you to store photos, videos, documents, and other content online and access them from any Apple device. It's the backbone of syncing data across your Apple ecosystem. With iCloud, all your devices stay updated automatically, ensuring that the content you save on one device appears on all your others, whether it's a Mac, iPhone, or iPad.

Here's how to set up iCloud and start syncing your data:

1. **Sign In to iCloud**:

- On your MacBook Air M4, go to **System Preferences** > **Apple ID**. If you're not already signed in, enter your Apple ID and password to sign in to iCloud.

- Once signed in, you'll see a list of options for what to sync across your devices, such as **Photos**, **Contacts**, **Calendars**, **Reminders**, **Notes**, and more.

2. **Choose What to Sync**:

- From the iCloud settings, check the boxes next to the items you want to sync. For example, if you want to sync your photos across all your Apple devices, ensure that **iCloud Photos** is enabled.

- To sync **Contacts**, **Calendars**, and **Notes**, just check their corresponding boxes.

3. **Accessing iCloud Content on Other Devices**:

- Any content that you sync via iCloud will automatically appear on your other Apple devices. For instance, any photo you take on your iPhone will appear in the **Photos** app on your MacBook Air M4 once iCloud Photos is enabled.

- Similarly, your contacts, calendars, and even Safari bookmarks will sync across all devices, ensuring you can access them no matter which device you're using.

4. **iCloud Drive**:

   o   iCloud Drive is a cloud storage service that lets you store documents, presentations, and other files in the cloud, just like Dropbox or Google Drive.

   o   To sync files via iCloud Drive, simply drag them into the **iCloud Drive** folder on your Mac. These files will then be available on any other device that's signed in to iCloud.

5. **iCloud Backup**:

   o   iCloud doesn't just sync files—it can also back up your devices. You can back up your iPhone or iPad data to iCloud, ensuring that all your apps, photos, and settings are safely stored and easily restored in case of data loss.

2. AirDrop: Instantly Share Files Between Apple Devices

AirDrop is one of the fastest and easiest ways to transfer files between Apple devices. Whether you're sending a photo from your iPhone to your MacBook Air M4 or sharing a document from your Mac to your iPad, AirDrop does it all with just a few taps or clicks.

Here's how to use AirDrop:

1. **Enable AirDrop**:

   o   On your MacBook Air M4, open **Finder** and click on **AirDrop** in the sidebar. Alternatively, you can click on the **Control Center** icon in the menu bar and select **AirDrop** to enable it.

o On your iPhone or iPad, swipe down from the top right corner to open the **Control Center**, then tap **AirDrop**. You can choose to allow AirDrop from **Contacts Only** or **Everyone**.

2. **Send Files via AirDrop**:

o On your MacBook Air M4, locate the file you want to share. Right-click it and choose **Share** > **AirDrop**. You'll see a list of nearby devices that are connected to AirDrop.

o Select the device you want to send the file to. For example, you might see your iPhone or an iPad in the list. After selecting the device, the recipient will receive a notification asking if they want to accept the file.

o On your iPhone or iPad, tap **Accept** to receive the file.

3. **Send Photos or Videos**:

o AirDrop works seamlessly with the **Photos** app as well. Open the **Photos** app on your iPhone or iPad, select the photo or video you want to share, and tap the **Share** button. Choose **AirDrop** from the options, then select your MacBook Air M4 to instantly send the file.

AirDrop works quickly and doesn't require an internet connection, making it ideal for transferring large files in an instant. It's especially useful when you're moving photos, videos, documents, or even app data across devices.

3. Universal Clipboard: Copy and Paste Across Devices

One of the most impressive features in the Apple ecosystem is **Universal Clipboard**, which allows you to copy content from one Apple device and paste it onto another. This feature works across your iPhone, iPad, and MacBook Air M4, so if you're working on a project on your iPhone, you can easily transfer the content to your MacBook with a simple copy-and-paste.

Here's how to use Universal Clipboard:

1. **Ensure iCloud is Set Up and Signed In**:

   o Universal Clipboard requires that all your devices be signed in to the same Apple ID with iCloud enabled. Make sure you've signed into iCloud on both your MacBook Air M4 and the device from which you want to copy content (e.g., your iPhone or iPad).

2. **Enable Bluetooth and Wi-Fi**:

   o Ensure that both **Bluetooth** and **Wi-Fi** are enabled on all devices you plan to use with Universal Clipboard. This is necessary for the devices to communicate and share content across the ecosystem.

3. **Copy on One Device**:

   o Simply copy content on one device as you normally would— this could be text, a link, or even an image. For example, on your iPhone, you can copy a paragraph of text or a link from Safari.

4. **Paste on Another Device**:

    o   Switch to your MacBook Air M4, open the app where you want to paste the content, and paste it as you would normally. The copied content from your iPhone will be available to paste directly onto your MacBook.

Universal Clipboard is incredibly useful for anyone working across multiple Apple devices. It allows for seamless transitions between devices without the need for additional apps or cables, making your workflow smoother and more efficient.

Using AirDrop and Universal Clipboard for Seamless Transfers

In today's fast-paced world, efficiency is key, and Apple's AirDrop and Universal Clipboard features are two of the best tools to make your MacBook Air M4 experience smoother and faster. Whether you're moving a file from your MacBook to your iPhone or copying a paragraph from your iPad to paste on your MacBook, these features are designed to keep things simple, quick, and completely seamless. Let's dive in and explore how you can use both AirDrop and Universal Clipboard to streamline your daily tasks.

AirDrop: Instantly Share Files Between Apple Devices

What is AirDrop? AirDrop is Apple's peer-to-peer file sharing feature that allows you to send photos, documents, videos, and more between Apple devices without the need for an internet connection or cables. It's like magic, but it's actually powered by Bluetooth and Wi-Fi technology. AirDrop automatically detects nearby devices, and as long as the devices are within close proximity, you can instantly send files back and forth.

How to Use AirDrop: Here's a step-by-step guide to help you start using AirDrop on your MacBook Air M4:

1. **Enable AirDrop on Your MacBook Air M4:**

    o Open **Finder** (the smiling face icon on your Dock).

    o In the Finder window, click on **AirDrop** from the sidebar.

    o If it's your first time using AirDrop, you may see a message prompting you to enable Bluetooth and Wi-Fi. Make sure both are turned on.

    o If your Mac is set to be discoverable only by Contacts, you can change this setting by clicking on **Allow me to be discovered by** and selecting **Everyone**. This will ensure that other devices can easily find your MacBook when you want to send or receive files.

2. **Send a File via AirDrop:**

    o Locate the file you want to share (whether it's a photo, document, or video).

    o Right-click (or Control-click) the file and select **Share**.

    o From the sharing options, select **AirDrop**.

    o Your Mac will start searching for nearby devices. The available devices will appear as icons on your screen.

    o Select the device you want to send the file to.

    o The recipient will receive a notification asking them to accept or decline the transfer. Once they accept, the file will be sent over instantly.

3. **Receive a File via AirDrop:**

    o If someone is sending you a file via AirDrop, you'll see an incoming notification on your MacBook.

    o Choose **Accept** to receive the file. It will be automatically saved in your **Downloads** folder, or you can specify a location where you'd like to store it.

    o AirDrop even allows you to receive files while your MacBook is asleep, as long as you have Wi-Fi and Bluetooth enabled.

Pro Tips for Using AirDrop:

- **Close Proximity**: AirDrop works best when the devices are within 30 feet of each other, so make sure both devices are nearby.

- **File Types**: AirDrop supports most file types, including photos, videos, contacts, PDFs, and more. However, there are a few restrictions on certain file types or sizes, so check the file's format if you're having trouble sending it.

- **AirDrop on iPhone/iPad**: To use AirDrop on your iPhone or iPad, simply swipe down from the top-right corner (on newer models) or swipe up from the bottom (on older models) to open the **Control Center**. Tap **AirDrop**, and choose either **Contacts Only** or **Everyone** to make your device discoverable.

Universal Clipboard: Copy and Paste Across Devices

What is Universal Clipboard? Universal Clipboard takes the seamless experience a step further by allowing you to copy content (text, images, links, etc.) from one Apple device and instantly paste it onto another, whether it's your MacBook, iPhone, or iPad. It works across your entire Apple ecosystem, meaning you can easily switch between devices without losing your clipboard data.

How Does Universal Clipboard Work? This feature uses the same Bluetooth and Wi-Fi technology as AirDrop to sync your clipboard data across Apple devices. As long as your devices are signed into the same Apple ID and within Bluetooth and Wi-Fi range, you can copy content from one device and paste it onto another. It's almost like your clipboard follows you, wherever you go.

How to Use Universal Clipboard:

1. **Ensure Devices Are Set Up Correctly:**

   o Make sure all your devices (MacBook, iPhone, iPad) are signed into the same **Apple ID**. This is crucial for Universal Clipboard to work properly.

   o Ensure **Bluetooth** and **Wi-Fi** are turned on for each device.

   o All devices should be relatively close to each other.

2. **Copy Content on One Device:**

   o On your MacBook, iPhone, or iPad, select the text, image, or link you want to copy.

   o On Mac, you can use **Command + C** to copy, or right-click and choose **Copy**. On iPhone/iPad, tap and hold the selected content and choose **Copy** from the context menu.

3. **Paste on Another Device:**

   o Switch to your other Apple device (for example, from your iPhone to your MacBook Air M4).

   o Place the cursor where you want to paste the content.

o On your Mac, use **Command + V** or right-click and select **Paste**. On iPhone/iPad, tap and hold the text field and select **Paste**.

o The content you copied from the first device will appear instantly on the second device.

Pro Tips for Using Universal Clipboard:

- **Limitations**: Universal Clipboard works across all Apple devices, but it has some limitations. The content remains on your clipboard for a short period (about two minutes), so you need to paste it on your second device quickly before it expires.

- **Great for Copying Links**: This feature is particularly useful for copying links from your phone and pasting them onto your MacBook Air M4 to open in a browser. You don't need to type the URL again; just copy and paste.

- **Works with Images and Text**: You can use Universal Clipboard for more than just text. Copy images, web links, or even screen grabs, and paste them across devices seamlessly.

Why AirDrop and Universal Clipboard Are Game-Changers

Together, AirDrop and Universal Clipboard make Apple's ecosystem incredibly powerful, especially for users who own multiple Apple devices. No more emailing files to yourself, no more cables to connect devices, and no more switching between apps to manually transfer content. With these two features, you can work more efficiently, stay organized, and share files faster than ever before.

Imagine this scenario: You're working on a document on your MacBook Air M4, and you realize you need a photo from your iPhone. Instead of manually uploading it to a cloud service or emailing it to yourself, you simply AirDrop it from your iPhone to your Mac. You continue editing your document, then copy a section of text from the web on your iPad and paste it directly into the document on your MacBook, all without skipping a beat.

It's all about simplifying your digital life and streamlining tasks that would otherwise take longer. These features are designed to help you stay connected and productive, no matter which Apple device you're using.

CHAPTER 11: WORKING WITH EXTERNAL DEVICES

Connecting External Monitors, Printers, and Accessories

The MacBook Air M4 offers a robust set of ports and wireless capabilities that allow users to easily connect external devices like monitors, printers, and storage drives. Whether you're looking to extend your workspace with an additional display, print important documents, or back up your data, this guide will walk you through everything you need to know to make these connections seamless.

Connecting an External Monitor

External monitors can greatly enhance your productivity, offering more screen real estate for multitasking, creative work, or presentations. Fortunately, connecting a monitor to your MacBook Air M4 is a straightforward process. Here's how to do it:

Step 1: Choose the Right Cable or Adapter The MacBook Air M4 comes with **two Thunderbolt 4 (USB-C)** ports, which are capable of driving external displays. Depending on the type of monitor you have, you may need an adapter:

- **HDMI Monitors**: If your monitor uses an HDMI port, you'll need a **USB-C to HDMI adapter** or a **USB-C to HDMI cable**.

- **DisplayPort Monitors**: For monitors with DisplayPort inputs, you can use a **USB-C to DisplayPort adapter** or a **USB-C to DisplayPort cable**.

- **USB-C Monitors**: If you're using a modern USB-C monitor, you can connect directly with a **USB-C to USB-C cable**.

Step 2: Connect the Cable to the Monitor and MacBook Air M4 Once you have the right cable or adapter, connect one end to your monitor and the other end to your MacBook Air M4's Thunderbolt port.

Step 3: Adjust Display Settings Once the monitor is connected, your MacBook Air should automatically detect it. If it doesn't, follow these steps:

1. Open **System Preferences** from the Apple menu.

2. Click on **Displays**.

3. Under the **Display** tab, you should see your monitor listed. If not, click **Detect Displays** to manually prompt your MacBook to search for the external monitor.

You can now adjust your display settings:

- **Mirror Displays**: This option duplicates your MacBook's screen onto the external monitor.

- **Extend Displays**: This gives you an extended desktop across both your MacBook and the external monitor, ideal for multitasking.

Choose the option that best suits your needs.

Step 4: Set the Resolution and Orientation If necessary, you can fine-tune the resolution, refresh rate, and orientation of the external monitor. Just click on the **Display** tab in **System Preferences** and select the **Scaled** option under the Resolution section. Choose the best resolution for your monitor.

Connecting a Printer

Printing from your MacBook Air M4 is as easy as connecting your printer either via **USB** or **Wi-Fi**. Here's how you can do both:

Step 1: Connect via USB If you have a USB printer, simply plug it into one of your MacBook's USB-C ports using a **USB-C to USB-A adapter**. After connecting, your MacBook should recognize the printer automatically. If it doesn't:

1. Go to **System Preferences** from the Apple menu.

2. Click on **Printers & Scanners**.

3. Click the + sign to add a printer.

4. Your printer should appear in the list. Select it and click **Add**.

Step 2: Connect via Wi-Fi To connect a printer over Wi-Fi, ensure your printer and MacBook Air are on the same Wi-Fi network. Many printers today support wireless printing via AirPrint, Apple's printing technology.

1. Ensure that your printer is powered on and connected to the same Wi-Fi network as your MacBook.

2. Open **System Preferences** and select **Printers & Scanners**.

3. Click the + sign to add a printer.

4. Your printer should appear under the **Default** tab. Select it and click **Add**.

If your printer doesn't support AirPrint, you might need to install the printer's software from the manufacturer's website. Simply follow the on-screen instructions for installing the necessary drivers.

Step 3: Print a Test Page To ensure everything is working properly, print a test page from any application. Open a document, click **File**, and select **Print**. Choose your printer from the list, adjust settings if needed, and hit **Print**.

Connecting External Storage Devices

External storage devices such as USB flash drives, external hard drives, or SSDs are perfect for expanding your MacBook Air M4's storage or for backing up your data. Here's how to connect these devices:

Step 1: Plug in the Storage Device If you have a **USB-A drive** (the traditional USB port), you'll need a **USB-C to USB-A adapter**. Plug the drive into the adapter, and then connect it to one of the MacBook's Thunderbolt 4 ports.

If you have a **USB-C drive**, simply plug it directly into the Thunderbolt 4 port.

Step 2: Access the Drive Once connected, your MacBook should recognize the external storage automatically. It will appear as an icon on your **Desktop** or under **Locations** in **Finder**.

Click on the icon to open the drive and start transferring files.

Step 3: Ejecting the Drive Always eject your external drive properly before unplugging it to prevent data corruption. To eject:

1. Drag the external drive's icon to the **Trash** (the Trash icon will turn into an eject symbol).

2. Alternatively, right-click (or Control-click) on the drive's icon and select **Eject**.

Troubleshooting Common Issues with External Devices

While connecting external devices to your MacBook Air M4 is generally easy, you may sometimes encounter issues. Here are some common problems and solutions:

1. The external monitor isn't displaying anything

- Ensure that the monitor is turned on and properly connected.

- Try using a different cable or adapter.

- Go to **System Preferences > Displays**, and click **Detect Displays** to manually search for the monitor.

2. Printer not showing up

- Ensure that your printer is properly connected to your network or USB port.

- For Wi-Fi printers, check if they are connected to the same network as your MacBook.

- Visit the printer manufacturer's website to download the latest drivers or software for macOS.

3. External drive not recognized

- Try unplugging the drive and plugging it into another port.

- Check the connection to ensure the drive is securely connected.

- Use **Disk Utility** (found in **Applications > Utilities**) to repair the disk if it's not showing up.

Using Your MacBook Air M4 for Video and Audio Editing

The **MacBook Air M4** isn't just for web browsing and word processing — it's also a surprisingly capable machine for video and audio editing. Thanks to the powerful **M4 chip**, this laptop can handle demanding tasks like **video editing, audio production**, and even **graphic design**, all while maintaining its sleek, ultra-portable form. Whether you're a beginner looking to edit your YouTube videos or a professional working on full-length films, the MacBook Air M4 is built to keep up with you. In this section, we'll explore how you can make the most of your MacBook Air M4 for creative tasks, optimize its performance for smooth editing, and ensure your work shines.

The Power of the M4 Chip in Creative Workflows

The heart of the MacBook Air M4's impressive performance is the **M4 chip**. Apple's custom silicon has transformed the MacBook Air into a powerhouse, especially for creative professionals. With **8-core CPU** and **10-core GPU** configurations, the M4 chip delivers exceptional speed, efficiency, and graphics performance, making it ideal for video and audio editing.

Why is the M4 chip so good for creative tasks?

- **Faster Rendering**: The M4 chip speeds up rendering times in video editing software like **Adobe Premiere Pro** or **Final Cut Pro**. Whether you're working with **4K video**, **multi-layer effects**, or **high-resolution audio**, the M4 chip handles complex rendering tasks with ease.

- **Enhanced GPU for Graphics**: Editing video often requires heavy graphics processing, especially when adding special effects or transitions. The **M4's 10-core GPU** enables **smooth playback** of high-resolution footage, even with color grading and other intensive tasks.

- **Unified Memory**: The M4 chip uses **unified memory**, meaning your MacBook doesn't need to constantly shuffle data between different parts of the system. This results in faster access to your video files, less lag, and smoother multitasking.

Overall, the M4 chip provides a **blazing-fast performance** for even the most demanding video and audio editing projects, making it a fantastic choice for creatives on the go.

Choosing the Right Software for Video and Audio Editing

To unlock the full potential of the MacBook Air M4 for video and audio editing, you'll need the right software. Fortunately, the MacBook Air M4 is compatible with a wide range of professional-grade tools for creative professionals. Here are a few options:

- **Adobe Premiere Pro**: One of the most popular video editing tools, **Premiere Pro** offers a comprehensive set of features for everything from basic edits to complex, multi-track edits. The MacBook Air M4's performance with Premiere Pro is smooth, thanks to the powerful **GPU acceleration** of the M4 chip.

- **Final Cut Pro**: If you're an Apple enthusiast or a professional editor, **Final Cut Pro** is a top choice. It's optimized for macOS, which means you get a **seamless experience** with faster rendering times, smooth playback, and excellent integration with other Apple software and services.

- **DaVinci Resolve**: If color grading is a significant part of your workflow, **DaVinci Resolve** is a must-have. With the MacBook Air M4's processing power, DaVinci Resolve can handle even complex color correction and grading tasks with ease.

- **GarageBand** and **Logic Pro X**: For audio editing, **GarageBand** is a fantastic free tool for beginners, while **Logic Pro X** offers more advanced features for professionals. Both work smoothly on the MacBook Air M4, thanks to the processing power of the M4 chip.

Tips to Optimize Your MacBook Air M4 for Video and Audio Editing

While the MacBook Air M4 is powerful on its own, there are several ways you can optimize your system to get the best performance out of your editing sessions.

1. **Keep Your macOS and Editing Software Updated**

Always make sure that your macOS and editing software are up to date. Updates often include performance improvements, bug fixes, and optimizations that can improve stability and performance. Enable **automatic updates** for macOS and keep an eye out for updates to your editing software.

2. **Use an External SSD for Video Storage**

Video files, especially in **4K** or **HD**, can take up a significant amount of space. To avoid running into storage limitations and slowing down your editing performance, consider using an **external SSD** for storing video files. SSDs provide much faster read/write speeds compared to traditional hard drives, ensuring quick access to large files.

3. **Free Up System Storage**

While the MacBook Air M4 comes with plenty of storage options, editing software and media files can quickly eat up that space. Make sure to regularly clean up your system by removing unused files and applications. Use macOS's **Storage Management** feature to identify and delete large files or apps that you no longer need.

4. **Increase RAM and Optimize Memory Usage**

The MacBook Air M4 comes with **8GB or 16GB of unified memory** (RAM), which is plenty for most video editing tasks. However, if you're working with very large projects, you may want to ensure that no other applications are running in the background while you're editing. Close unnecessary apps and background processes to free up memory for your editing software.

5. **Use Proxy Files for Smooth Editing**

When working with high-resolution footage (such as 4K video), editing can be sluggish because your MacBook has to process large video files. **Proxy files** are lower-resolution copies of your video clips that allow you to edit more smoothly. Once you've completed your edits, you can replace the proxy files with the original high-res footage for final rendering.

6. **Disable Background Apps and Notifications**

Before diving into an intensive editing session, disable background apps and notifications that may interrupt your workflow. You can do this by using **Focus Mode** or manually closing any apps that aren't needed. This minimizes distractions and ensures that all of your MacBook's resources are focused on the editing process.

7. **Monitor System Performance with Activity Monitor**

If you notice any lag or performance hiccups, open the **Activity Monitor** to see which processes are using the most CPU or memory. This can help you identify any apps or background tasks that are consuming system resources and potentially affecting your editing performance.

Managing External Devices for Video and Audio Editing

While your MacBook Air M4 is a capable machine, you'll likely need to connect external devices to maximize your workflow. Here are a few devices that can enhance your editing experience:

- **External Monitors**: Having a second display can greatly improve your editing workflow by providing more screen real estate. The MacBook Air M4 supports **external monitors** via its Thunderbolt/USB-C ports, allowing you to extend your workspace.

- **External Audio Interfaces**: For high-quality audio recording, use an **external audio interface** such as **Focusrite Scarlett** or **PreSonus AudioBox**. These devices allow you to connect professional microphones, instruments, and audio equipment to your MacBook Air M4 for superior sound quality.

- **External Storage Drives**: As mentioned earlier, an external **SSD** or **HDD** can significantly improve your editing experience, especially when working with large video files. Look for drives with fast transfer speeds, such as those with **Thunderbolt 3** support, to ensure seamless data access.

- **USB-C Hubs**: The MacBook Air M4 features **two Thunderbolt 3 (USB-C)** ports, which are perfect for connecting multiple devices at once. A **USB-C hub** will allow you to connect your external drives, audio interfaces, and monitors all through a single port, keeping your setup clean and organized.

Rendering and Exporting: Making the Most of Your MacBook Air M4's Performance

Once your project is complete, rendering and exporting is the final step. The MacBook Air M4's M4 chip allows you to render your videos quickly without compromising on quality. Here are a few tips to improve your rendering times:

1. **Choose the Right Export Settings**: Be mindful of your export settings. If you're not delivering 4K footage, exporting in **1080p** can significantly reduce rendering time without sacrificing quality.

2. **Render in Stages**: If you're working with a complex video project, consider rendering in stages. This reduces the strain on your MacBook and can help you spot errors early in the process.

3. **Use Hardware Acceleration**: Both **Final Cut Pro** and **Premiere Pro** support **hardware acceleration**, which uses your MacBook's GPU to speed up rendering. Make sure this option is enabled to get the best performance.

Gaming on the MacBook Air M4: Performance and Graphics

The MacBook Air M4 has long been known for its sleek, ultra-portable design, exceptional battery life, and robust performance for everyday tasks. But what about gaming? If you're a casual gamer or someone who occasionally enjoys a gaming session, you might be wondering how well the MacBook Air M4 holds up when it comes to running modern games. Let's dive in and explore the gaming performance of this powerhouse, focusing on the M4 chip and the integrated graphics.

1. The M4 Chip: Powering Your Gaming Experience

At the heart of the MacBook Air M4 lies the revolutionary M4 chip. Apple's custom-designed silicon brings a world of improvements to MacBook users. The M4 chip is equipped with a powerful CPU, GPU, and Neural Engine, all working in harmony to deliver exceptional performance. While the MacBook Air M4 isn't necessarily designed as a high-end gaming machine, its M4 chip offers significant improvements over previous Intel-based MacBook models, especially when it comes to graphics processing.

The **GPU** within the M4 chip has been optimized for efficiency and performance. It's capable of handling light to moderate gaming with ease, offering good frame rates and smooth visuals. For casual gaming, this makes the MacBook Air M4 a surprisingly capable device for most popular titles.

2. Graphics Performance: A Seamless Gaming Experience

When it comes to graphics, Apple has made substantial strides in integrating its own GPU into the M4 chip. Although the MacBook Air M4 does not feature a dedicated, high-performance GPU like its Pro or Max counterparts, the integrated graphics within the M4 chip are more than capable for casual gaming. Games that rely on a combination of both CPU and GPU power will run smoothly, with stunning visuals and fluid motion.

The MacBook Air M4 offers good performance with games that don't have high graphics demands. Titles like **Fortnite**, **Minecraft**, and **Stardew Valley** will run effortlessly at high settings, providing an immersive experience without compromising frame rates. On the other hand, more graphically demanding games like **Cyberpunk 2077** or **Shadow of the Tomb Raider** might require adjustments to settings to maintain smooth gameplay.

The key to maximizing gaming performance is balancing **graphics settings**. For smoother performance on the MacBook Air M4, you might need to adjust settings like resolution, texture quality, and effects. Lowering some of these settings can help maintain a consistent and playable frame rate, especially for AAA games that demand more from the hardware.

3. Games That Run Smoothly on the MacBook Air M4

Let's get into some of the best games that the MacBook Air M4 handles well. The M4 chip, with its efficiency and performance optimizations, opens up a world of gaming possibilities:

Casual and Indie Games

- **Stardew Valley** – This beloved farming simulator runs perfectly on the MacBook Air M4. It's a light game that requires minimal resources but delivers hours of fun with vibrant graphics and an engaging storyline.

- **Minecraft** – Whether you're building a fortress or exploring vast landscapes, Minecraft runs smoothly at high settings on the M4-powered MacBook Air. The game's blocky graphics are easy for the M4 GPU to handle, and the gameplay is fluid.

- **Celeste** – This indie platformer is visually beautiful yet low on system requirements. The MacBook Air M4 handles its pixel art-style graphics and fast-paced gameplay with ease.

Popular Multiplayer Games

- **Fortnite** – The MacBook Air M4 handles Fortnite well, especially when graphics settings are adjusted to medium. The game runs smoothly with a stable frame rate, allowing you to enjoy intense battles with no lag.

- **League of Legends** – A favorite for gamers worldwide, League of Legends is a game that is highly optimized for various systems. On the MacBook Air M4, you can expect smooth gameplay at medium-high settings, providing an enjoyable experience in fast-paced multiplayer matches.

- **Rocket League** – This fast-paced game that combines soccer with acrobatic vehicles runs surprisingly well on the MacBook Air M4. Set the graphics to medium, and you'll have a great gaming experience.

Simulation and Strategy Games

- **The Sims 4** – Whether you're building houses or creating virtual stories, The Sims 4 is a great game for the MacBook Air M4. The game's casual gameplay and low-to-moderate graphical demands make it a perfect fit.

- **Civilization VI** – This strategy game works well on the MacBook Air M4, although you might need to adjust settings for higher frame rates. The slower-paced nature of this game means it's easier to handle for the M4 chip without much performance loss.

4. Optimizing Settings for a Better Gaming Experience

Now that you know which games run well on your MacBook Air M4, let's focus on optimizing your settings to get the best possible gaming experience. The MacBook Air M4 can deliver good performance, but the key to maximizing it lies in making smart adjustments to settings. Here are a few tips:

Adjust Game Settings for Optimal Performance

For graphically demanding games, it's always a good idea to dial down some of the more intensive settings:

- **Resolution** – Lowering the resolution will boost performance. Try lowering it to 1080p or lower, depending on the game, for smoother gameplay.

- **Texture Quality** – Reducing the texture quality can make a significant impact on performance without sacrificing too much visual fidelity.

- **Shadow and Effect Quality** – Shadows and complex effects (like reflections and dynamic lighting) can be very demanding. Lowering these settings will give you a performance boost with minimal effect on the gameplay experience.

Turn Off Unnecessary Background Processes

Before starting your game, make sure to close unnecessary applications running in the background. This will free up system resources and ensure that the game gets as much power as possible. You can use **Activity Monitor** (found in Applications > Utilities) to check and close any unnecessary processes eating up CPU and memory.

Keep Your MacBook Air M4 Cool

Gaming can generate heat, and with the MacBook Air M4 being a thin and lightweight laptop, it's essential to keep it cool. Overheating can lead to throttling, where the system reduces its performance to manage the heat. Ensure that your MacBook has adequate ventilation by keeping it on a hard surface. You can also invest in a laptop cooling pad to help with temperature management during long gaming sessions.

Enable Low Power Mode When Needed

If you're concerned about battery life while gaming, enabling **Low Power Mode** can help conserve energy. Keep in mind, however, that this might slightly reduce performance, so it's best used when you're playing less graphically demanding games.

5. The Verdict: Is the MacBook Air M4 a Gaming Machine?

While the MacBook Air M4 isn't designed to be a dedicated gaming laptop, its powerful M4 chip and integrated graphics provide a surprisingly good gaming experience for casual and indie games. Titles that are less resource-intensive will run smoothly, and with some adjustments, even more demanding games can be playable. If you're someone who enjoys gaming as a hobby, you'll find the MacBook Air M4 capable of handling a wide range of titles.

For gamers who prioritize high-performance, cutting-edge graphics, you may want to look toward higher-end machines like the MacBook Pro M4 or other dedicated gaming laptops. But for everyday gaming and casual sessions, the MacBook Air M4 delivers excellent value, offering solid performance without the bulk.

Gaming on the MacBook Air M4 can be an enjoyable experience as long as you're mindful of your game settings and the occasional performance tweak. It might not replace a dedicated gaming PC, but for many users, it's more than enough to dive into some fun, immersive worlds.

How to Connect to Wi-Fi Networks and Troubleshoot Connectivity

Your MacBook Air M4 is designed to connect to Wi-Fi effortlessly, but sometimes, you might run into a few bumps along the way. Whether you're trying to connect to a new Wi-Fi network or troubleshooting an existing one, this section will guide you through the process with easy-to-follow steps and tips to improve your Wi-Fi experience.

Connecting to Wi-Fi Networks

Getting connected to Wi-Fi on your MacBook Air M4 is a simple process, and once you're set up, it's smooth sailing. Here's how to connect your MacBook Air M4 to a Wi-Fi network:

1. **Turn on Your MacBook Air M4**: First, power up your MacBook if it's not already on. Wait for the desktop to load, and ensure that macOS is fully up and running.

2. **Access Wi-Fi Settings**:
   In the top-right corner of your screen, you'll find the Wi-Fi icon. It looks like a series of curved lines stacked on top of each other. If the icon is grayed out, it means you are not yet connected to any Wi-Fi network. Click on the Wi-Fi icon to open the Wi-Fi menu.

3. **Select Your Network**:
   Once the menu is open, you'll see a list of available Wi-Fi networks. These are the networks within your range, whether it's your home network, a public Wi-Fi spot, or a network at work. Find and click on the name of your Wi-Fi network.

4. **Enter the Password**:
   If your network is password-protected (which it should be), a prompt will appear asking for the Wi-Fi password. Enter it carefully—note that passwords are case-sensitive. Once you've entered the correct password, click **Join**.

5. **Confirmation of Connection**:
   After a few moments, your MacBook will connect to the Wi-Fi network. The Wi-Fi icon will turn black, indicating that you are successfully connected. You'll also see a notification if you're connected to the internet.

MACBOOK AIR M4 USER GUIDE

At this point, you're all set to start browsing, streaming, or working from your MacBook Air M4!

Troubleshooting Common Connectivity Issues

While Wi-Fi connections on the MacBook Air M4 are usually smooth, occasionally, you might encounter some hiccups. Here's how to troubleshoot and fix common issues.

1. Wi-Fi Won't Connect or Keep Disconnecting

This can be a frustrating problem, especially when you need a stable connection. Here's what you can do:

Step   1:   Check   Your   Wi-Fi   Router
First, make sure that the issue isn't with the Wi-Fi router. Is your router turned on? Is it plugged in properly? Try restarting your router by turning it off for about 10 seconds and then turning it back on. This can often resolve temporary connectivity issues.

Step   2:   Forget   the   Network   and   Reconnect
Sometimes, the connection may be "stuck." Go to **System Preferences > Network > Wi-Fi**. Click on the "Advanced" button, where you'll see a list of saved networks. Select your Wi-Fi network and click -" to forget it. Now, return to the Wi-Fi menu at the top of the screen and try connecting again by selecting your network and entering the password.

Step   3:   Restart   Your   MacBook
If your MacBook is still not connecting after trying the above steps, restart

your computer. Sometimes a quick reboot can help fix any software glitches or temporary issues preventing Wi-Fi from connecting.

Step   4:   Check   for   Software   Updates
In some cases, outdated macOS software can cause connectivity issues. To check for updates, click on the **Apple menu** in the top left of your screen and select **About This Mac > Software Update**. If there are updates available, install them. This can often resolve underlying bugs causing Wi-Fi issues.

Step   5:   Check   Wi-Fi   Settings   on   the   Router
If the issue persists, check your router settings. Ensure that the router is not set to a mode incompatible with your MacBook (such as a different Wi-Fi frequency band). You may need to access the router's admin page to adjust settings. You can refer to your router's manual or the support website for instructions on how to do this.

2. Weak Signal or Slow Internet Speeds

If your Wi-Fi connection is working, but the signal is weak or the internet is slow, it's a good idea to check a few things:

Step   1:   Move   Closer   to   the   Router
Physical obstructions such as walls, metal objects, or even appliances can interfere with the Wi-Fi signal. If you're too far away from the router, you might experience weak or intermittent signals. Try moving closer to the router to see if your connection improves.

Step   2:   Switch   to   a   5   GHz   Network   (If   Available)
Many modern routers offer both 2.4 GHz and 5 GHz networks. The 5 GHz

band typically provides faster speeds and less interference than the 2.4 GHz band. If your router supports it, try connecting to the 5 GHz network for improved performance. In the Wi-Fi menu, check to see if there are multiple network options and connect to the 5 GHz one.

Step 3: Check for Interference from Other Devices Other electronics in your home, such as microwaves, baby monitors, or even neighboring Wi-Fi networks, can cause interference. Try moving your router away from other electronic devices and changing the Wi-Fi channel in your router's settings if necessary.

Step 4: Use a Wi-Fi Extender or Mesh Network If your home is large or the router is far from where you work, consider investing in a Wi-Fi extender or mesh network. These devices can help boost the signal and provide more reliable coverage throughout your home or office.

3. Wi-Fi Connection Keeps Dropping

If your MacBook is consistently disconnecting from Wi-Fi, the problem could be related to software settings, network congestion, or issues with the router:

Step 1: Reset Your Network Settings Sometimes, network settings may become corrupted, which can lead to dropped connections. To reset them, go to **System Preferences > Network**, select **Wi-Fi**, and click the minus button to remove it. Then, click the plus button, select Wi-Fi, and reconnect to your network. This will refresh your network settings.

Step   2:   Check   Your   Router's   Firmware
Outdated router firmware can cause connectivity issues, including frequent disconnections. Log into your router's admin panel and check for any available firmware updates. The process for updating firmware varies by router brand, so refer to your router's manual or manufacturer's website for detailed instructions.

Step   3:   Check   for   Network   Congestion
If many devices are connected to your Wi-Fi, it may become congested, causing slowdowns or frequent disconnects. Try disconnecting unnecessary devices and see if that improves the stability of your connection.

4. General Wi-Fi Performance Tips

To get the most out of your MacBook's Wi-Fi performance, follow these additional tips:

- **Enable Auto-Join**: If your MacBook isn't automatically connecting to known networks, go to **System Preferences > Network > Wi-Fi > Advanced**. Ensure that the **Auto-Join** option is checked for your preferred networks.

- **Reduce Background App Usage**: If your MacBook is running multiple apps that use the internet (like streaming videos, cloud backups, or updates), it could slow down your Wi-Fi connection. Close any unnecessary apps to free up bandwidth.

- **Use Ethernet for Stable Connection**: If you need a more stable connection, consider using a USB-C to Ethernet adapter to connect directly to your router. This will bypass Wi-Fi interference and provide a faster, more reliable connection.

- **Check DNS Settings**: Slow internet can sometimes be caused by DNS issues. You can change your DNS server to a faster one, such as Google's DNS (8.8.8.8) or Cloudflare's (1.1.1.1). Go to **System Preferences > Network > Advanced > DNS**, and add the preferred DNS servers.

CHAPTER 12: YOUR MACBOOK AIR M4 FOR EDUCATION AND WORK

How the MacBook Air M4 Can Support Your Studies or Professional Tasks

Whether you're a student diving into a semester of intense studies or a professional handling complex tasks, the **MacBook Air M4** is designed to be your ideal companion. From its slim profile to its powerful M4 chip, this laptop is more than capable of supporting your daily tasks—whether you're writing essays, doing research, attending video meetings, or managing projects. In this section, we'll explore how the MacBook Air M4 can help you stay productive, organized, and efficient in both educational and professional settings.

Portability: A Lightweight Powerhouse

One of the standout features of the **MacBook Air M4** is its portability. If you're a student hopping from one lecture hall to another or a professional moving between meetings, this MacBook is designed to be lightweight and ultra-thin without compromising performance. Weighing just **2.7 pounds** (1.24 kg) and measuring only **0.63 inches** (1.61 cm) in thickness, the

MacBook Air M4 easily slips into any bag, making it perfect for on-the-go productivity.

Whether you're studying at the library, working from a coffee shop, or traveling between offices, the **MacBook Air M4** won't weigh you down. Its portability allows you to carry it with you all day, so you're always ready to dive into your work or learning material. Forget the days of lugging around a bulky laptop or feeling constrained to a desk—this MacBook is designed to adapt to your lifestyle, providing comfort without sacrificing power.

Battery Life: Stay Powered Up All Day

In education and work, time is precious, and there's nothing more frustrating than having your laptop run out of battery just when you're deep into a project or lecture. Fortunately, the **MacBook Air M4** excels in this area, offering impressive **battery life**. With up to **15 hours of wireless web browsing** and **18 hours of video playback**, the MacBook Air M4 can easily carry you through a full day of work or study without needing to be plugged in.

For students, this means you can attend back-to-back lectures, take notes, and research without worrying about finding an outlet during class. For professionals, this means you can attend virtual meetings, work on presentations, and review documents without constantly scrambling for your charger. Whether you're at home, on campus, or in a coffee shop, you can count on your MacBook Air M4 to keep you powered throughout the day. The long battery life ensures you stay productive no matter where life takes you.

Performance: Ready for Any Task

Under the sleek exterior of the **MacBook Air M4** lies a powerhouse designed for both efficiency and speed. The **M4 chip** powers through everyday tasks with ease, offering **exceptional performance** for everything from note-taking and research to video editing and coding. The MacBook Air M4's impressive **8-core CPU** and **10-core GPU** work together to handle multiple applications without breaking a sweat. Whether you're writing a research paper in **Microsoft Word**, conducting in-depth research in a **browser**, or analyzing data in **Excel**, this MacBook can handle it all.

For students who rely heavily on multitasking, the MacBook Air M4 offers seamless transitions between apps. You can have multiple tabs open, switch between research documents, and take notes without experiencing any lag. The **macOS Sequoia** operating system also ensures a smooth user experience, with optimizations that make navigating between applications intuitive and efficient. The **16GB of unified memory** also ensures that the MacBook can handle large files and demanding apps, so students can run research programs, coding environments, and media editing software without slowing down.

Video Conferencing: Perfect for Online Classes and Meetings

In the era of remote learning and virtual work environments, **video conferencing** has become an essential part of both education and work. Whether you're attending an online lecture, participating in a Zoom meeting, or conducting a virtual interview, the **MacBook Air M4** is designed to offer a smooth video conferencing experience.

The **12MP Center Stage webcam** is a significant upgrade, offering clearer and more vibrant video quality. It automatically adjusts the frame, keeping you centered as you move around during a video call. This makes attending virtual classes, meetings, and discussions a more immersive and professional experience. Paired with the laptop's **studio-quality microphone** and **spatial audio speakers**, your audio and video will be crisp and clear, ensuring that you're always heard and seen—whether it's a study group or a client meeting.

For students, this means no more worrying about blurry, low-quality video when attending online classes. For professionals, it means looking sharp during video calls with clients, colleagues, or superiors. The **MacBook Air M4** offers excellent performance for video conferencing, even in environments where background noise might be a concern. With its high-quality mic and speaker setup, you'll always have clear communication, whether you're discussing a group project or negotiating a business deal.

Note-Taking and Research: A Seamless Workflow

Whether you're writing notes during a lecture, brainstorming for an essay, or conducting research for a work project, the **MacBook Air M4** is an ideal companion for note-taking and research. Thanks to the responsive **Magic Keyboard**, typing long documents and notes feels natural, comfortable, and quick. The key travel is satisfying, and the layout is optimized for a smooth typing experience, which makes writing papers, essays, or meeting notes much easier.

The **Retina display** is another highlight, offering clear text and vibrant colors for your work. When researching, whether it's reading articles, viewing documents, or watching instructional videos, the MacBook Air M4's display provides a bright, sharp, and immersive experience. This is especially helpful for students who need to read long textbooks or review documents for hours on end.

For professionals, the **MacBook Air M4** is perfect for managing large documents, spreadsheets, and presentations. Whether you're analyzing data in Excel, creating reports in Word, or designing presentations in PowerPoint, the MacBook Air M4 can handle it all. Its performance is ideal for multitasking, so you can run multiple apps without worrying about lag, whether you're researching, writing, or managing a project at the same time.

Collaboration and File Sharing: Work Together Effortlessly

Collaboration is at the heart of both educational and professional tasks. The **MacBook Air M4** excels in this area by seamlessly integrating with the **Apple ecosystem**. If you're working on a group project, sharing files or collaborating in real time is as simple as ever. With **iCloud**, you can store your notes, research documents, and files securely and access them across all your Apple devices. Share files, folders, and documents with classmates, teammates, or colleagues with just a few clicks.

For professionals, this level of integration is invaluable. You can instantly share documents with colleagues, collaborate on projects in **Pages** or **Numbers**, and access your work from anywhere via **iCloud Drive**. Whether it's a team project or client work, the seamless file sharing and collaboration capabilities make teamwork easy and efficient.

Productivity Apps for Education and Work

Whether you're a student juggling assignments and deadlines, or a professional managing multiple projects and meetings, the MacBook Air M4 is packed with features that can help you boost your productivity and keep you on track. One of the biggest strengths of macOS is the wide range of apps designed to support your workflow—making your tasks more efficient and organized. In this chapter, we'll take a look at the best productivity apps available for both education and work, helping you navigate your day with ease.

1. Microsoft Office 365: The Go-To Suite for Work and Study

When it comes to productivity, **Microsoft Office 365** is likely the first name that comes to mind. It's not just for professionals—it's an essential tool for students too. The suite includes Word, Excel, PowerPoint, Outlook, OneNote, and more, making it a comprehensive solution for all your document creation, data analysis, presentations, and email management needs.

- **Word**: Perfect for writing essays, research papers, reports, and anything that requires text-heavy documentation. The tools within Word, like built-in templates, spell-check, and formatting options, ensure that your documents look polished.

- **Excel**: A powerful tool for managing data. Whether you're tracking personal budgets, conducting research, or organizing projects, Excel's spreadsheets make managing large amounts of information much easier. You can create detailed graphs, run complex formulas, and analyze data without the hassle.

- **PowerPoint**: Whether it's for class presentations or work meetings, PowerPoint allows you to design visually stunning slideshows with ease. With customizable templates and seamless integration of multimedia, you can engage your audience more effectively.

- **OneNote**: Ideal for organizing notes across different subjects, projects, or meetings. OneNote syncs across devices, so whether you're taking notes on your MacBook or on your phone, you'll never lose track of important information.

- **Outlook**: A full-featured email client with excellent integration for managing your schedule, contacts, and emails. It's great for professionals, especially when you need to keep communication with clients, colleagues, and professors in one place.

Why It's Great for You: Office 365 is a tried-and-true suite that provides everything from writing papers to managing data. Plus, with cloud integration, your files are always accessible no matter where you are.

2. Notion: The All-in-One Workspace

Notion is quickly becoming a fan-favorite among students and professionals alike. It's an all-in-one workspace that combines notes, tasks, databases, calendars, and project management into a single, sleek interface. This makes it a powerful tool for anyone who needs to organize their work, class notes, and to-do lists efficiently.

- **Notes & Databases**: Organize your notes by subject, create databases for your assignments or work tasks, and keep everything in one place. You can easily categorize and tag your notes, making them easier to find later.

- **Task Management**: Use Notion's customizable task management tools to stay on top of your assignments, meetings, and projects. Set deadlines, add priorities, and track your progress in a visually appealing dashboard.

- **Collaborative Features**: If you're working on a group project, Notion allows you to collaborate with others in real-time, making it easy to share notes, track progress, and keep everything organized in one shared space.

Why It's Great for You: Whether you're managing a research project, keeping track of tasks, or jotting down lecture notes, Notion's flexibility makes it an essential app for staying organized, focused, and productive.

3. Evernote: Your Digital Notebook

For those who prefer a simple, easy-to-use note-taking app with strong organizational features, **Evernote** is a solid choice. This app is designed to capture all your ideas, tasks, and notes in a format that's simple to access and search.

- **Text, Audio, and Image Notes**: Evernote allows you to take notes in multiple formats, from typed text to voice memos, to attaching images and PDFs. This makes it easy to capture everything from lecture notes to meeting minutes.

- **Search and Tags**: Evernote makes it incredibly easy to find what you're looking for, even if you have thousands of notes. You can search within the text of your notes and organize them using tags for better categorization.

- **Syncing Across Devices**: Like OneNote, Evernote syncs across your devices, meaning that your notes are accessible whether you're on your MacBook, phone, or tablet.

Why It's Great for You: Evernote is perfect for anyone who needs a digital notebook to keep everything from class notes to ideas for projects in one easy-to-search place. The multi-device syncing ensures you never have to worry about losing access to your work.

4. Trello: Visual Project Management

If you're working on projects—either in school or professionally—**Trello** is an excellent tool for managing tasks visually. It uses a board and card system that allows you to easily track the progress of your projects and organize tasks.

- **Kanban Boards**: Trello's Kanban-style boards allow you to break down your projects into manageable tasks. You can create boards for different projects, and within each board, add cards for specific tasks, assign deadlines, and move cards between lists to track progress.

- **Collaboration**: Trello's real-time collaboration features allow you to invite others to your boards. This makes it great for group projects, team collaborations, or even work tasks.

- **Checklists and Due Dates**: You can create checklists within cards and set due dates to ensure tasks are completed on time. It's simple, but incredibly effective for staying organized.

Why It's Great for You: Trello is perfect for those who prefer a visual, drag-and-drop approach to project management. Whether you're coordinating a group assignment or managing multiple tasks at work, Trello keeps everything in one place and allows you to stay on top of deadlines.

5. Google Keep: Quick Notes and Reminders

For those who prefer simplicity, **Google Keep** is a fantastic app to quickly jot down ideas or create reminders. It's an easy-to-use note-taking app that's especially helpful for students who need to capture ideas or reminders on the go.

- **Simple Notes**: You can quickly take text, voice, or photo notes and add labels for better organization. Keep is perfect for capturing fleeting thoughts, to-do lists, or ideas you don't want to forget.

- **Reminders and Color-Coding**: Google Keep allows you to set reminders for notes, ensuring you stay on top of important tasks. You can also color-code your notes to keep different types of information organized.

- **Integration with Google Drive**: Keep integrates seamlessly with Google Drive, so you can easily save and share your notes with others. This makes it a convenient option for collaborative projects.

Why It's Great for You: Google Keep is ideal for anyone who needs to quickly capture notes or reminders without the complexity of other apps. It's fast, efficient, and syncs with your Google account for easy access across devices.

Organizing Documents and Files with Finder and Spotlight

As you settle into your new MacBook Air M4, one of the most powerful tools you'll have at your fingertips for staying organized is **Finder**. Finder is essentially your file management system, and it's where you'll be spending a lot of time, especially as you accumulate more documents, projects, and files over time. But, no need to worry—macOS offers a range of tools and techniques to make sure you never feel lost in a sea of documents again. Let's dive into the ways you can keep your files neatly organized and easy to access using **Finder** and **Spotlight**.

Getting to Know Finder: Your File Management Hub

When you open Finder, you're looking at the gateway to all your documents and files on your MacBook Air M4. Think of it like the filing cabinet of your computer, but way more powerful and intuitive. Finder is simple to use, but it offers so many ways to customize it to your needs. Here's how to get started:

1. The Finder Window: A Quick Overview

When you open **Finder**, you'll see a window with several key components:

- **Sidebar**: On the left side, you'll see links to your folders, devices, and locations like iCloud Drive, Downloads, Documents, Applications, and more. This sidebar is your quick-access menu. You can add or remove any folders or locations you use most often to keep them handy.

- **File Viewer**: In the main area of the window, you'll see all the files and folders within the selected location. The files will appear as icons or a list, depending on the view you prefer.

- **Toolbar**: At the top, the toolbar contains useful buttons for things like creating new folders, managing files, and changing how your files are displayed.

2. Sorting Files in Finder

To keep everything neat, sorting your files is a must. Fortunately, Finder makes it simple:

- **Sort by Name**: This is the most common way to keep your files in order, especially when dealing with a lot of documents. Just click the "Name" column in Finder to sort them alphabetically.

- **Sort by Date**: If you prefer to keep your files organized by the most recent or oldest, click the "Date" column to sort by when the files were last modified.

- **Sort by Type or Size**: You can also organize your files by file type (e.g., PDF, Word, Excel) or size. This is great for sorting documents based on their format or identifying which files are taking up the most space on your MacBook.

You can also customize your Finder to show files in specific ways, like **icons** or **list view**. If you're working on a project that involves a lot of similar files (like research papers or notes), you can switch to **Column View** for easy file navigation and previewing.

3. Using Tags for Easy File Identification

One of the most underrated features of Finder is the ability to use **Tags** to categorize and color-code your files. Tags are like virtual highlighters that can help you quickly spot important documents or files related to a specific project. Here's how you can use them:

- **Assigning Tags**: Right-click on any file or folder in Finder and choose a color tag. You can even add custom tags like "Important," "To Review," or "Completed."

- **Customizing Tags**: Want to create your own system? Head to **System Preferences > Tags**, and you can rename, reorder, or add custom tags to suit your needs.

- **Searching by Tags**: Tags make searching for files in Finder so much easier. If you've tagged all your work-related documents as "Work," you can simply click the "Work" tag in the sidebar to view everything related to that project.

Organizing Files into Folders: The Basics of Structure

While Finder's sorting and tagging features are powerful, keeping your files organized into logical, easy-to-navigate folders is the best way to ensure everything stays tidy in the long run.

1. Create Folders to Group Related Files

Think of **folders** as the main structure of your file organization system. You can create folders based on categories like "School," "Work," or "Personal Projects." To create a new folder, simply press **Command + Shift + N** or right-click and select **New Folder**. You can also create subfolders inside larger folders, like a "Work" folder that contains subfolders for different projects.

- **Naming Folders**: Give each folder a clear and concise name, like "Math Research" or "Project X Files," so you know exactly what's inside without having to open it.

- **Color-Coding Folders**: You can assign color tags to folders as well, just like you do with files. This adds an extra layer of organization and makes it easy to spot certain folders at a glance.

2. Smart Folders: Automatically Organize Files

For more advanced organization, you can create **Smart Folders** in Finder. These are folders that automatically update to include files that meet certain criteria, such as file type or keywords. For example, you could create a Smart Folder that gathers all your PDF files or all your documents related to a specific project.

To create a Smart Folder:

1. Open Finder and go to **File > New Smart Folder**.

2. Use the search bar to filter files by file type, modification date, or keywords.

3. Save the Smart Folder, and it will automatically update with relevant files as you work.

Spotlight Search: Your Quick Access Tool

While Finder is great for organizing and sorting, sometimes you just need to find a file quickly without sifting through multiple folders. That's where **Spotlight** comes in.

Spotlight is an incredibly fast search tool built into your MacBook Air M4, and it's ideal for quickly locating any file, document, or app on your computer. Here's how to use it effectively:

1. Using Spotlight to Search for Files

- Press **Command + Space** to bring up Spotlight (or click on the magnifying glass in the top-right corner of your screen).

- Start typing the name of the file you're looking for. Spotlight will search through all of your files and documents, including those stored in iCloud, for a match.

- Spotlight also displays suggestions for apps, emails, and even web searches based on your query. If you're looking for a document, it will show up in the search results along with the app you used to open it.

2. Narrowing Your Search

Spotlight is great at finding files quickly, but you might want to narrow down your results further. To do this:

- **Search by file type**: Type a file extension into Spotlight, such as ".pdf" or ".docx", and it will only show files with that extension.

- **Use Keywords**: If you've used tags for your files, Spotlight will also pull up files with matching tags. For example, if you've tagged your files as "Urgent," typing "Urgent" in Spotlight will show you all the files with that tag.

3. Searching Using Natural Language

The best part about Spotlight is that it understands natural language. You can type things like:

- "Documents modified last week"

- "Photos from vacation"

- "Emails from John Doe"

Spotlight will sort through your documents, emails, and files to give you what you're looking for based on the phrases you type.

4. Using Spotlight for Apps and Settings

In addition to searching for files, you can also use Spotlight to find apps or open system preferences. For example, typing "Safari" opens the Safari browser, while typing "System Preferences" opens up the system settings where you can adjust your MacBook's settings.

CHAPTER 13: THE MACBOOK AIR M4 IN THE APPLE ECOSYSTEM

Integrating with Your iPhone, iPad, and Apple Watch

Apple's ecosystem is built around the idea of seamless integration across its devices, and the MacBook Air M4 is at the heart of that experience. Whether you're using an iPhone, iPad, or Apple Watch, your MacBook can work effortlessly with these devices to make your daily tasks easier, more efficient, and more enjoyable.

This chapter will walk you through how to make the most of Continuity features such as **Handoff**, **AirDrop**, and **Universal Control**, and how they can help you stay connected and productive across all your Apple devices. Think of these features as a bridge that connects everything in your Apple world, allowing you to transition smoothly between devices without missing a beat.

What Is Continuity?

Continuity is the term Apple uses to describe how its devices work together to offer a smooth, seamless experience. It allows your MacBook Air M4 to automatically detect and work with your iPhone, iPad, or Apple Watch. This integration extends across a variety of apps and functions, so you can pick up where you left off without worrying about device compatibility or interruptions. Continuity brings the magic of Apple's ecosystem to life.

Handoff: Pick Up Where You Left Off

One of the standout features of Continuity is **Handoff**. Have you ever started drafting an email on your iPhone and wished you could finish it on your MacBook Air M4? Or maybe you're browsing a website on your iPad and want to switch to your MacBook to read an article in more detail? That's where Handoff comes in.

How Handoff Works: Handoff allows you to start a task on one Apple device and pick it up on another without skipping a beat. Whether you're working on an email, browsing the web, writing a document, or even composing a message, Handoff will show you a little icon on your other Apple devices, signaling that you can pick up where you left off.

Here's how to use Handoff:

1. **Enable Handoff**: Make sure that all your devices are signed in with the same Apple ID and connected to the same Wi-Fi network. On your MacBook Air M4, go to **System Preferences > General** and check the box for "Allow Handoff between this Mac and your iCloud devices."

2. **Start a Task**: Start your task on your iPhone or iPad. For example, if you're writing an email in the Mail app or browsing Safari, your device will store the task in the background.

3. **Switch to Your MacBook**: On your MacBook Air M4, look for the Handoff icon in the app dock. You'll see a small icon of the app you were using, like a Safari tab or an email draft.

4. **Continue on Mac**: Click the icon to instantly jump to that task on your MacBook, and you're good to go!

Use Case Example: Let's say you're composing a long email on your iPhone. Halfway through, you realize you need to add some attachments and do more detailed formatting, but you'd rather use your MacBook's larger screen and keyboard. Thanks to Handoff, you can open the Mail app on your MacBook and continue typing right where you left off on your iPhone.

AirDrop: Send Files Instantly Across Devices

One of the most useful features in the Apple ecosystem is **AirDrop**. It's a fast, wireless way to send files between your devices without the need for email, cloud storage, or cables. Whether you're sending photos, videos, documents, or website links, AirDrop makes it easy to share files from your MacBook Air M4 to your iPhone, iPad, or Apple Watch (though the Apple Watch has more limited file handling).

How to Use AirDrop: AirDrop is incredibly simple to use. Here's a quick guide on how it works:

1. **Enable AirDrop**: Make sure AirDrop is turned on. On your MacBook, open **Finder**, click **AirDrop** in the sidebar, and set it to "Allow me to be discovered by: Contacts" or "Everyone." On your iPhone or iPad, swipe up from the bottom to open the **Control Center** and tap on the AirDrop icon. Set it to "Everyone" or "Contacts Only."

2. **Select the Files**: On your MacBook Air M4, select the file you want to share. This could be an image, a document, or even a webpage you want to send to your iPhone or iPad.

3. **Send via AirDrop**: Right-click on the file and select **Share > AirDrop**. Your nearby Apple devices will appear in the AirDrop menu. Select the device you want to send the file to, and the transfer will begin instantly.

4. **Receive on iPhone/iPad**: On your iPhone or iPad, you'll see a pop-up asking if you want to accept the file. Once you tap **Accept**, the file will automatically save to the appropriate app, such as Photos, Notes, or Files.

Use Case Example: Imagine you're working on a presentation on your MacBook and want to quickly share a few slides with a colleague using their iPhone. Instead of going through email or cloud storage, simply AirDrop the slides. They'll instantly appear on their phone, ready to be viewed, with no need for any cables or extra steps.

Universal Control: Master Multiple Devices with One Mouse and Keyboard

Universal Control is a game-changing feature for users who own multiple Apple devices, such as a MacBook Air M4, iPad, and even another Mac. It allows you to use your MacBook's mouse and keyboard to control your iPad or another Mac seamlessly. You can even drag and drop files between devices as if they were part of one big desktop.

How to Use Universal Control:

1. **Enable Universal Control**: First, make sure that your MacBook Air M4, iPad, and any other Apple devices are signed into the same Apple ID. On the Mac, go to **System Preferences > Displays** and click **Universal Control**. Check the options to "Allow your cursor and keyboard to move between any nearby Mac or iPad."

2. **Place Your Devices Side-by-Side**: Arrange your MacBook Air M4 and iPad on your desk so they're physically next to each other, or place them on opposite sides of your screen, depending on where you want the cursor to travel.

3. **Move the Cursor Between Devices**: With Universal Control enabled, just move your mouse pointer to the edge of the MacBook screen, and it will smoothly transition to your iPad. You can click, drag, and drop files between devices just as you would if they were part of the same screen.

Use Case Example: If you're working on a report on your MacBook Air M4, but you want to draw some diagrams or take notes on your iPad, you can simply move your cursor from your Mac to your iPad. Use your MacBook to type and your iPad to sketch. You can even drag files from the MacBook directly into an app on the iPad, like dragging a PDF into the Notes app to annotate.

Why This Integration Matters

These features are not just about convenience; they are about enhancing productivity and creativity. By integrating your MacBook Air M4 with your other Apple devices, you create a unified workspace where the lines between devices blur. Tasks that would normally require multiple steps across different apps or even platforms are simplified and streamlined. This integration allows you to focus on what truly matters—getting your work done, staying connected, and making the most of the tools at your disposal.

Example Scenario: Imagine you're working on a project, switching from an iPhone for a quick message reply, to your MacBook to write a report, and then to your iPad to take notes or draw diagrams. All this happens without losing context or having to repeat any steps. It's like having a supercharged, flexible workspace that adapts to how you work best.

Syncing Photos, Files, and Notes across Devices

In today's fast-paced world, staying connected across your devices is essential, and Apple's ecosystem makes this incredibly easy. The seamless synchronization of photos, files, and notes between your MacBook Air M4 and other Apple devices, like your iPhone, iPad, or Apple Watch, is powered by iCloud. It ensures that all your important content is readily available, no matter where you are or which device you're using. This chapter will walk you through the process of syncing photos, files, and notes, helping you maintain a unified experience across your Apple devices.

What is iCloud?

Before diving into syncing, let's first understand what iCloud is. iCloud is Apple's cloud storage service that allows you to store your photos, documents, notes, and more securely in the cloud. Once content is stored on iCloud, you can access it from any device that is connected to the same iCloud account—whether that's your MacBook Air M4, your iPhone, or your iPad.

What's even better is that iCloud automatically keeps your content up-to-date across devices. So, if you add a photo on your iPhone, it will instantly appear on your MacBook Air M4, and vice versa. No more worrying about manually transferring files between devices or losing track of content!

How to Set Up iCloud on Your MacBook Air M4

Setting up iCloud on your MacBook Air M4 is simple. Here's how you can get started:

1. **Open System Preferences**:

   o On your MacBook Air M4, click on the **Apple Menu** (□) at the top-left corner of your screen and select **System Preferences**.

2. **Sign in with Your Apple ID**:

   o In the System Preferences window, find and click on **Apple ID**. If you're not signed in, you'll be prompted to enter your Apple ID and password. This is the same Apple ID you use on your iPhone, iPad, and any other Apple devices.

3. **Enable iCloud Services**:

   o After signing in, click on **iCloud** in the sidebar. Here, you'll see a list of services that you can sync using iCloud, such as **Photos, iCloud Drive**, **Notes**, and others.

   o Make sure to check the box next to **Photos, iCloud Drive**, and **Notes** (or any other services you wish to sync). This ensures that your content is automatically stored and synced with iCloud.

4. **Storage and Settings**:

- At the bottom of the iCloud panel, you'll see your iCloud storage usage. If you need more storage space, click on **Manage** to see options for upgrading your storage plan.

- You can also manage individual app syncing here. For instance, if you only want to sync **Photos** but not **Mail**, you can uncheck the box next to **Mail** to free up iCloud space.

Syncing Photos Across Devices

One of the most valuable features of iCloud is the ability to sync photos seamlessly across your devices. Whether you're snapping a picture on your iPhone or editing a photo on your MacBook, iCloud ensures everything stays up to date. Here's how to make sure your photos are synced:

1. **Enable iCloud Photos on Your MacBook Air M4**:

   - Open the **Photos** app on your MacBook Air M4.

   - In the menu bar at the top, click on **Photos**, then select **Preferences**.

   - Under the **iCloud** tab, check the box next to **iCloud Photos**. This will start syncing your entire photo library with iCloud.

   - You can choose to either **Download Originals to this Mac** or **Optimize Mac Storage**. If you choose the latter, your photos will be stored in full resolution on iCloud, but your MacBook will only keep smaller, space-efficient versions, saving you local storage space.

2. **Syncing Between iPhone and iPad**:

    o On your iPhone or iPad, open the **Settings** app.

    o Tap your name at the top, then select **iCloud**.

    o Scroll down and ensure **Photos** is toggled on. This will ensure that any photos you take on your iPhone or iPad will automatically upload to iCloud and sync with your MacBook Air M4.

3. **Accessing Your Photos**:

    o Once iCloud Photos is enabled, any changes you make to your photos on one device—whether editing, adding, or deleting—will automatically sync across all your devices. You can view and manage your entire photo library from the **Photos** app on your MacBook, iPhone, and iPad.

Syncing Files Across Devices with iCloud Drive

iCloud Drive is your go-to solution for syncing and managing documents across devices. Whether you're working on a Word document, a PDF, or a spreadsheet, iCloud Drive keeps all your files in sync and accessible from any Apple device.

1. **Enable iCloud Drive on Your MacBook Air M4**:

    o In **System Preferences**, click on **Apple ID**, then select **iCloud**.

- Make sure **iCloud Drive** is checked. This will enable iCloud Drive to sync your documents and files across all Apple devices.

2. **Organizing Files in iCloud Drive**:

   - Open the **Finder** on your MacBook and select **iCloud Drive** from the sidebar. This will display all the files and folders stored in iCloud.

   - You can create folders, drag and drop files, and organize them as needed. Any changes made here will be reflected across your other Apple devices.

3. **Syncing Files on Your iPhone and iPad**:

   - On your iPhone or iPad, open the **Settings** app.

   - Tap your name, then go to **iCloud** and toggle on **iCloud Drive**.

   - You can access your synced files by opening the **Files** app on your iPhone or iPad. Any file saved to iCloud Drive on your MacBook will show up here.

4. **Accessing Files Across Devices**:

   - With iCloud Drive, you can access your files from any device connected to your iCloud account. Simply open the **Files** app on your iPhone or iPad, and navigate to **Browse** > **iCloud Drive** to find your files.

o   You can open documents, edit them, and they will be automatically saved to iCloud, ready to be accessed from any other device.

Syncing Notes Across Devices

If you're using Notes to jot down ideas or keep track of important information, iCloud ensures that your notes are always in sync, no matter which device you're using.

1. **Enable iCloud Notes on Your MacBook Air M4**:

    o   Open **System Preferences**, click on **Apple ID**, and select **iCloud**.

    o   Ensure **Notes** is checked to sync your notes across devices.

2. **Using Notes on iPhone and iPad**:

    o   On your iPhone or iPad, go to **Settings** > [your name] > **iCloud**.

    o   Make sure **Notes** is toggled on.

3. **Creating and Accessing Notes**:

    o   Open the **Notes** app on any of your devices. Whether you're on your MacBook, iPhone, or iPad, your notes will appear automatically, and any edits will sync across all devices.

- o You can even create folders to organize your notes, and iCloud ensures that everything stays up-to-date no matter where you are.

Managing Syncing Settings

While iCloud works automatically in the background, it's a good idea to periodically review your settings to ensure everything is syncing the way you want it.

1. **Check iCloud Settings**:

   - o On your MacBook Air M4, go to **System Preferences** > **Apple ID** > **iCloud** to manage what gets synced.

   - o You can enable or disable syncing for specific apps, like Photos, Notes, and iCloud Drive, depending on your needs.

2. **Freeing Up iCloud Storage**:

   - o If your iCloud storage is getting full, go to **System Preferences** > **Apple ID** > **iCloud** > **Manage** to see what's taking up space.

   - o You can delete old files or upgrade your storage plan if needed.

Using Handoff, Universal Control, and AirDrop for a Smooth Experience

Apple's ecosystem is a powerful feature that seamlessly integrates all its devices, creating a unified experience across iPhones, iPads, Macs, and even Apple Watches. The MacBook Air M4, with its advanced capabilities, is designed to make these integrations smoother than ever, allowing users to switch between devices effortlessly. In this section, we'll delve into three essential features — **Handoff**, **Universal Control**, and **AirDrop** — explaining how they help you move between Apple devices with ease, streamline your daily tasks, and make your workflow more efficient.

Handoff: Seamless Continuity Between Devices

What is Handoff? Handoff is a feature that allows you to start a task on one Apple device and pick it up on another without missing a beat. This could mean starting an email on your iPhone and finishing it on your MacBook Air M4, or beginning a document on your iPad and continuing to edit it on your MacBook Air M4. Handoff takes advantage of your devices being linked through iCloud, so they know what you're working on, regardless of which device you started with.

How Does Handoff Work? When you're signed into iCloud on multiple Apple devices, Handoff works automatically. You don't have to do anything special to set it up; simply start using an app, and it will show up on your other devices. For example, if you open Safari on your MacBook Air M4 and start browsing a page, you can easily continue browsing on your iPhone by swiping up from the bottom of the lock screen, where Safari will appear with the same webpage.

Use Case Scenario: Let's say you're working on an email on your iPhone while commuting to work. You start typing the subject, but realize you need to attach some documents from your MacBook. As soon as you sit down at your desk with your MacBook Air M4, the email you were writing will appear in the Mail app on your MacBook. All you need to do is click on it, finish composing, and attach your files. No need to search through your iPhone's mail app or waste time copying and pasting text. It's a smooth transition that saves time and effort.

Handoff isn't limited to just emails or documents either. It works with many apps, including Safari, Mail, Messages, Notes, Pages, and more. The flexibility it offers allows you to be productive on the go, without feeling tethered to one device.

Universal Control: Effortlessly Control Multiple Devices

What is Universal Control? Universal Control is a feature that takes the integration between your Apple devices a step further by allowing you to control multiple devices with a single keyboard and mouse (or trackpad). If you have an iPad or a second Mac, Universal Control lets you use your MacBook Air M4's keyboard and trackpad to control the other device seamlessly.

How Does Universal Control Work? The beauty of Universal Control is how fluidly it lets you move between devices. If you have your MacBook Air M4 and an iPad nearby, for example, simply move your cursor from one device's screen to the other, and the cursor will follow. You can drag and drop files from your MacBook to your iPad and vice versa, just like they're part of the same screen. This is all done wirelessly, and no additional setup is required — it just works.

Use Case Scenario: Imagine you're a designer who works with both a MacBook and an iPad to sketch out ideas. With Universal Control, you can use your MacBook's keyboard and trackpad to control the iPad's screen without having to touch the iPad. You can drag images from your MacBook to the iPad or copy text from a document and paste it directly into a drawing app on the iPad. This ability to easily switch between devices is a game-changer for multitaskers or creatives who need to work across multiple devices simultaneously.

For example, if you're writing a report on your MacBook Air M4 but want to annotate some graphics or images on your iPad, Universal Control makes it effortless. You can drag the graphic from your MacBook, drop it onto your iPad's screen, make your annotations, and drag it back to your MacBook—all using a single keyboard and trackpad. The ease of use makes Universal Control an essential tool for improving efficiency and productivity.

AirDrop: Fast and Easy File Sharing

What is AirDrop? AirDrop is Apple's method of quickly transferring files between devices over a short distance, using both Bluetooth and Wi-Fi.

Whether you need to send a photo, a document, or even a whole folder, AirDrop makes the process quick and easy, without the need for cables or an internet connection. All you need is your MacBook Air M4 and another Apple device nearby.

How Does AirDrop Work? To use AirDrop, both devices need to have AirDrop enabled. On your MacBook Air M4, open Finder, then click on "AirDrop" in the sidebar. The app will show a list of nearby devices that are also using AirDrop. To send a file, simply drag and drop it onto the icon of the device you want to send it to. On the receiving device, a notification will appear asking if you want to accept the file. Once accepted, the file will be transferred almost instantaneously.

Use Case Scenario: Imagine you're editing a presentation on your MacBook Air M4 and need to quickly send it to your colleague who's using an iPhone. Instead of emailing the file or using a cloud service, you can simply use AirDrop to transfer the file. It's much faster and more convenient. You don't even need to worry about internet connections or slow upload/download times—AirDrop just works instantly as long as both devices are close to each other.

Another scenario is when you're on the go and you capture a beautiful photo on your iPhone. You can instantly AirDrop it to your MacBook Air M4 for further editing in Photoshop, or directly into your presentation. No cables, no waiting. It's a seamless, frictionless way to move files between devices quickly.

The Apple Ecosystem: A Unified Experience

By using **Handoff**, **Universal Control**, and **AirDrop**, the MacBook Air M4 becomes an integral part of the broader Apple ecosystem. These features work together to ensure that all your Apple devices work in harmony, allowing you to switch between them without missing a beat.

Whether you're working on a project, editing photos, or simply moving files, these features eliminate the need for complicated processes, making your workflow faster and more efficient. They are perfect examples of how Apple's ecosystem enhances your productivity, allowing you to stay in the flow regardless of which device you're using.

Incorporating these features into your daily routine is not just about using technology—it's about enhancing your experience, making your devices work for you, and removing friction from your tasks. Once you get used to this seamless integration, you'll wonder how you ever worked without it.

CHAPTER 14: CONCLUSION

Summary: The MacBook Air M4 in Your Daily Life

The **MacBook Air M4** is more than just another laptop; it's a seamless blend of performance, portability, and practicality. Apple has long been known for creating devices that not only look good but also work exceptionally well, and the MacBook Air M4 is no exception. For those who value a lightweight, ultra-portable device without compromising on power, the MacBook Air M4 is a game-changer. In this chapter, we'll explore how this laptop fits into your daily life, making tasks easier, faster, and more enjoyable.

Portability: Take Your Power Anywhere

If there's one thing that sets the MacBook Air M4 apart from many other laptops, it's its **portability**. Weighing just around 2.7 pounds and measuring less than 0.6 inches thick, it's one of the lightest laptops in its class. Whether you're a student rushing between classes, a professional hopping from one meeting to the next, or a traveler with limited luggage space, the MacBook Air M4 is built for life on the go.

This portability isn't just about its size; it's about the fact that you don't have to sacrifice performance for it. Apple's M4 chip delivers power that rivals many desktop computers, so you can work on your projects, watch movies, or edit photos and videos without worrying about lag or performance slowdowns, even when you're on a train or in a coffee shop. With such a compact design, it fits easily into backpacks and bags, and you can carry it around all day without ever feeling weighed down.

Performance: More Power Than Ever Before

While the MacBook Air has always been known for its portability, what really elevates the M4 model is its **performance**. Powered by the new **M4 chip**, this MacBook delivers a faster, smoother experience than its predecessors. The M4 chip is built to handle demanding tasks with ease, such as video editing, graphic design, and coding, while still delivering exceptional energy efficiency.

For everyday tasks like browsing the web, checking emails, or working on documents, the MacBook Air M4 feels lightning-fast. It boots up in seconds, apps launch instantly, and switching between multiple tabs or programs is a breeze. Whether you're using it for productivity, creativity, or entertainment, you'll notice the difference in performance compared to older models or other laptops in the same category.

It's also worth noting that the M4 chip is specifically designed to work in harmony with macOS, providing smooth performance with minimal effort. This integration ensures that the MacBook Air M4 is optimized for everything you do, making it the perfect companion for both work and play.

Battery Life: Power That Lasts All Day

Another key feature that makes the MacBook Air M4 stand out is its **battery life**. Apple promises up to 18 hours of video playback and up to 15 hours of web browsing on a single charge. In real-world usage, this means you can easily get through an entire workday without needing to plug in. Whether you're in the middle of a meeting, on a long flight, or simply lounging at home, the MacBook Air M4 has you covered.

The impressive battery life is thanks to the M4 chip's energy efficiency. Even though it delivers high-end performance, it's designed to consume less power, meaning you get more out of every charge. This is a significant advantage for users who are always on the move and need a laptop that can keep up with their busy schedules.

Overall User Experience: Everything You Need, Nothing You Don't

The **MacBook Air M4** isn't just a powerful machine; it's designed to provide an exceptional **user experience** from start to finish. From the moment you open the box, you're greeted with a device that feels premium. The Retina display, with its stunning colors and sharp resolution, makes everything you do feel more immersive, whether you're reading, watching videos, or browsing the web.

The **keyboard** is comfortable and responsive, perfect for long typing sessions. Plus, the **trackpad** is large and precise, offering an intuitive way to navigate through macOS. Whether you're swiping through apps, zooming in on a photo, or scrolling through a webpage, everything feels natural and effortless.

The MacBook Air M4 also integrates seamlessly into the **Apple ecosystem**, allowing you to sync your content across devices. Whether you're moving files between your iPhone, iPad, or MacBook, the process is quick and painless with features like **Handoff**, **AirDrop**, and **Universal Clipboard**.

For those who need additional security, the **Touch ID** feature allows you to easily unlock your MacBook and make payments with a simple fingerprint scan. It's a small but important feature that adds an extra layer of convenience and safety.

Finally, the MacBook Air M4 is perfect for anyone who needs a machine that works well with both personal and professional tasks. Whether you're attending virtual meetings, creating presentations, working on spreadsheets, or watching the latest Netflix series, the MacBook Air M4 does it all without skipping a beat.

Why the MacBook Air M4 Is Perfect for Most Users

When you combine **portability**, **performance**, **battery life**, and **user experience**, the MacBook Air M4 emerges as the **ultimate laptop** for most users. It's not just for tech enthusiasts or professionals; it's for anyone who needs a device that can keep up with the fast pace of modern life.

For students, it's the perfect tool for note-taking, research, and completing assignments. For professionals, it's an efficient workhorse that can handle everything from office tasks to complex creative work. And for casual users, it's a lightweight and sleek device that provides the entertainment and productivity needed in daily life.

What makes the MacBook Air M4 truly special is how it balances these elements. Apple has created a laptop that works for everyone—no matter your needs or lifestyle. Whether you're a student, a professional, a content creator, or someone who simply enjoys a good movie or a video call with family, the MacBook Air M4 adapts to your life, making it easier, more efficient, and more enjoyable.

In conclusion, the **MacBook Air M4** is a device that effortlessly fits into your daily routine, providing power when you need it, portability when you're on the go, and a user experience that's second to none. It's a laptop that works for you, so you can focus on what matters most.

Final Tips and Tricks to Enhance Your Experience

Now that you've gotten to know your MacBook Air M4 inside and out, let's dive into some final tips and tricks that will help you elevate your experience and truly unlock the full potential of your device. Whether you're a seasoned Mac user or new to the world of Apple, these tips will make your daily tasks smoother, your workflows faster, and your overall experience more enjoyable.

Here are some advanced features, shortcuts, and tools to optimize performance, save time, and take your MacBook Air M4 to the next level:

1. Master Keyboard Shortcuts

If you're looking to boost productivity and speed up your workflow, mastering keyboard shortcuts is one of the easiest and most effective ways to do so. Here are a few that will save you countless minutes every day:

- **Command + Space**: Open **Spotlight Search** instantly. This is your go-to for finding files, apps, and even performing quick calculations or web searches without opening a browser.

- **Command + Tab**: Quickly switch between open apps. If you have multiple programs running, this shortcut lets you flip between them faster than ever. No more fumbling around with the mouse!

- **Command + H**: Hide the current window. If you're in an app and don't want to minimize it, simply use this shortcut to hide it, leaving your desktop or another app in full view.

- **Command + Shift + 4**: Take a screenshot of a specific area on your screen. Once you press these keys, your cursor will turn into a crosshair, and you can drag to capture exactly what you need.

- **Command + Option + Esc**: Force quit an app that's not responding. If an app freezes up, don't stress—this shortcut is your emergency exit for closing unresponsive applications quickly.

By mastering these shortcuts and incorporating them into your daily routine, you'll shave off a lot of time that would otherwise be spent navigating menus or clicking around.

2. Utilize Mission Control and Multiple Desktops

When you're juggling multiple projects or apps, having a cluttered screen can slow you down. Luckily, **Mission Control** is here to save the day. This macOS feature allows you to organize your windows in a way that's both intuitive and effective:

- **Mission Control**: Swipe up with three fingers (or press **F3**) to activate Mission Control. This shows you all your open windows at a glance, helping you to quickly find what you need.

- **Multiple Desktops**: With **Mission Control**, you can create multiple virtual desktops. Simply drag a window to the top of the screen, where it'll create a new desktop space. This is great if you want to keep certain apps open but separated from your main workspace—perfect for keeping your personal and work apps organized.

Once you start using multiple desktops, you'll wonder how you ever lived without them. You can easily switch between desktops by swiping left or right with three fingers. It's like having multiple monitors, all without the extra physical setup.

3. Customize the Touchpad Gestures for Better Navigation

The MacBook Air M4's touchpad is one of the best out there, offering a variety of gestures to help you navigate with ease. But did you know you can customize the touchpad gestures to better suit your needs? Here are some gestures and tweaks to enhance your experience:

- **Trackpad Preferences**: Go to **System Preferences** > **Trackpad** to customize gestures. For example, you can set up a three-finger swipe to switch between full-screen apps or open Mission Control. You can even adjust the sensitivity of the touchpad to your liking.

- **Tap to Click**: If you prefer a lighter touch, turn on **Tap to Click** under **Trackpad Settings**. This allows you to tap the touchpad instead of pressing it, saving time and reducing strain on your fingers.

- **Right Click**: By default, the MacBook Air M4 supports **right-click** with two fingers. You can change this setting to your preference, whether you want it on the right or left side of the trackpad.

Once you get the hang of these gestures, you'll find that navigating through macOS becomes faster and more intuitive. Plus, customizing the touchpad to fit your style adds a personal touch to your device.

4. Manage and Optimize Startup Items

A common frustration for users is that MacBooks can feel slow to start up, especially if you have a lot of apps set to launch when you log in. Fortunately, you can easily manage and reduce the number of startup items to speed up your boot time:

- **System Preferences** > **Users & Groups** > **Login Items**: Here, you'll see a list of apps that open automatically when you start up your Mac.

MACBOOK AIR M4 USER GUIDE

Disable any apps you don't need to open right away by selecting them and clicking the minus (-) button.

This small tweak can make a noticeable difference in how quickly your MacBook Air M4 boots up, letting you get to work faster without waiting for unnecessary programs to load.

5. Take Advantage of iCloud and Handoff for Seamless Device Syncing

One of the best things about owning a MacBook Air M4 is how well it integrates with the rest of the Apple ecosystem. With **iCloud** and **Handoff**, you can keep all your devices in sync and move between them with ease.

- **iCloud**: Make sure iCloud is set up so that your documents, photos, and files are automatically synced across your devices. This is especially helpful if you're working across multiple Apple devices like an iPhone, iPad, or Apple Watch. You can access your files anywhere, anytime, without worrying about losing data.

- **Handoff**: With Handoff, you can start a task on one device and pick it up on another. For example, if you're composing an email on your iPhone, you can instantly finish it on your MacBook Air M4. Simply open the app on your Mac, and you'll see a notification to continue the task.

These features will streamline your workflow and make your life easier, as you can seamlessly transition between devices without losing any progress.

6. Organize Files Efficiently with Tags and Stacks

With so many files and apps on your MacBook Air M4, keeping things organized can become a challenge. Luckily, macOS offers powerful organization tools like **Tags** and **Stacks** to help keep your digital life in order:

- **Tags**: You can assign color-coded tags to your files and folders, making them easy to identify and group together. For example, use a red tag for urgent tasks or a green tag for completed projects. You can then search or filter by these tags in Finder for quicker access.

- **Stacks**: Stacks automatically organize files on your desktop into groups based on file type, date, or tags. To activate Stacks, right-click on your desktop and select **Use Stacks**. This is a great way to keep your desktop clean and make it easier to find files without sifting through clutter.

7. Use Night Shift and True Tone for a Healthier Screen Experience

Spending hours in front of your MacBook can take a toll on your eyes, but fortunately, macOS has built-in features that can reduce eye strain:

- **Night Shift**: This feature adjusts your screen's color temperature to warmer tones in the evening, reducing blue light exposure. To enable it, go to **System Preferences** > **Displays** > **Night Shift** and set it to turn on automatically at sunset.

- **True Tone**: If your MacBook Air M4 has True Tone, it automatically adjusts the screen's color balance to match the lighting in your environment. This results in a more natural viewing experience and can reduce eye fatigue during long working hours.

8. Back Up Your Data Regularly with Time Machine

Lastly, never underestimate the importance of backing up your data. If something were to go wrong with your MacBook Air M4, you'd want to make sure you have a reliable backup to restore from:

- **Time Machine**: Use Time Machine to back up your Mac regularly. It's easy to set up and will automatically create incremental backups of your entire system. This means you can restore individual files or your entire system if something goes wrong.

To set it up, just plug in an external hard drive, go to **System Preferences > Time Machine**, and follow the prompts. Remember, a regular backup could save you a lot of stress in the future.

Resources for Ongoing Learning and Support

Even though your journey with the MacBook Air M4 has just begun, there's a wealth of resources available to ensure you continue to get the most out of your device. Whether you're looking to explore new features, troubleshoot a tricky problem, or simply discover hidden tips and tricks, there's no shortage of help available. The world of macOS is vast, but with the right tools, you can navigate it with ease. Let's explore some of the best resources where you can keep learning and get assistance when needed.

1. Apple's Official Support Website

Apple's **official support website** is the first stop for most MacBook Air M4 users. Whether you're experiencing an issue or just want to learn more about a specific feature, the support site offers a treasure trove of information. Here, you'll find detailed guides, troubleshooting steps, and answers to common questions.

- **URL**: https://support.apple.com

- **What you'll find**:

    o **Step-by-step troubleshooting guides** for common issues like Wi-Fi problems, battery life issues, and software glitches.

    o **User manuals** for macOS and your MacBook Air M4, explaining everything from basic setup to advanced features.

    o **Downloadable software updates** and detailed instructions on how to keep your device secure and running smoothly.

Not only does this site offer support articles, but it also features interactive tools that can help you with diagnostics. If the problem isn't something you can fix with a simple guide, Apple Support allows you to schedule a call, chat with a representative, or even set up an appointment at your nearest Apple Store for in-person help.

2. Apple Communities

The **Apple Support Communities** is a great place to connect with other MacBook Air M4 users and get advice from fellow Apple enthusiasts. It's a vast, user-driven forum where you can ask questions, share tips, and learn from others who've had similar experiences.

- **URL**: https://discussions.apple.com

- **What you'll find**:

    - **User-driven discussions** where people share their experiences with problems they've encountered and how they solved them.

    - **Troubleshooting tips** for a wide range of issues, from basic macOS settings to more complex software and hardware problems.

    - **Searchable threads** on virtually every Apple product and service, including the MacBook Air M4, so chances are, if you have a question, someone else has already asked it and gotten an answer!

One of the best things about the Apple Communities is the variety of experience levels. Whether you're a seasoned pro or a first-time Mac user, you'll find answers that match your level of expertise. You might even stumble upon helpful user-created guides that explain things in a way that clicks for you.

3. YouTube Channels

YouTube is an excellent resource for visual learners who prefer to see things in action. There are countless channels dedicated to MacBook tutorials, tips, and troubleshooting advice. Some of the best YouTube creators offer in-depth, easy-to-understand tutorials on everything from getting started with macOS to using advanced features of your MacBook Air M4.

Here are a few YouTube channels that are particularly valuable:

- **Apple Support**: The official Apple Support YouTube channel offers concise tutorials on how to get the most out of your MacBook Air M4, with videos on everything from basic setup to exploring specific features of macOS.

    o **Channel link**: Apple Support YouTube

- **MacMost**: This is one of the most popular channels for Mac users, offering tips, tricks, and troubleshooting guides specifically for macOS and all Apple devices. The channel has content that caters to all experience levels.

    o **Channel link**: MacMost

- **iJustine**: While iJustine is known for her tech unboxings and reviews, she also creates user-friendly tutorials and guides for all things Apple, including macOS and MacBook-specific advice.

    o **Channel link**: iJustine

These channels offer high-quality, visual guides that walk you through features step-by-step. You can find everything from basic tutorials to more advanced tips and tricks to optimize your MacBook experience.

4. Third-Party Blogs and Communities

Sometimes, the best way to dive deeper into macOS is through **third-party blogs and websites** that specialize in Mac-related content. These sites often offer a fresh perspective and practical advice that's not available from official Apple resources.

- **MacRumors**: A long-time go-to site for everything Apple, MacRumors offers news, reviews, and guides for users who want to stay up-to-date with the latest macOS features and updates.

  - **Website link**: MacRumors

  - **What you'll find**:

    - **In-depth analysis** of new macOS features and updates.

    - **Troubleshooting tips** for solving complex problems.

    - **User comments and discussion** that often provide additional insights into common issues.

- **9to5Mac**: Another excellent source for breaking news, product reviews, and detailed guides on how to use macOS and Apple products effectively. They also post tutorials that are tailored to different user levels.

- o **Website link**: 9to5Mac

- **The Sweet Setup**: This site offers practical advice on how to set up your MacBook for various uses, from productivity to creativity. It's full of useful tips and software recommendations to help you get the most out of macOS.

  - o **Website link**: The Sweet Setup

These blogs often feature articles that dive deep into how to customize macOS, discover hidden features, and optimize your MacBook for better performance. They also offer expert advice on which apps and tools will make your workflow more efficient.

5. Online Courses and Tutorials

For users who want to take their macOS skills to the next level, **online learning platforms** like **Udemy**, **LinkedIn Learning**, and **Coursera** offer in-depth courses on macOS and the MacBook Air M4.

- **Udemy**: Udemy has several courses that cover everything from the basics of macOS to more advanced workflows for Mac users. These courses are usually taught by experienced instructors and include video lectures, quizzes, and practical exercises.

  - o **Course link**: Udemy - macOS Courses

- **LinkedIn Learning**: Formerly known as Lynda.com, LinkedIn Learning offers a range of video tutorials specifically designed to help users get the most out of macOS and their Apple devices. The courses are often aimed at professional development and can help you integrate macOS into your work environment.

- o **Course link**: LinkedIn Learning

These platforms can be especially helpful if you're someone who prefers structured learning and enjoys going deeper into specific aspects of macOS.

6. Apple Store and AppleCare Support

If you run into issues that you can't solve with online resources, don't hesitate to visit your local **Apple Store** or **Apple Authorized Service Providers**. They offer in-person support for hardware and software-related issues, and you can even book appointments with **Geniuses** for hands-on help.

- **Book an appointment**: Apple Genius Bar

- **AppleCare**: If you have AppleCare, you get priority support, extended warranty, and repairs. AppleCare support can be accessed via phone, chat, or email.

Apple's in-person support is one of the best aspects of owning Apple devices, offering direct help from highly trained professionals who know the system inside out.

MACBOOK AIR M4 USER GUIDE